Johnny Unitas

by JOEL H. COHEN

Illustrated with Photographs

Cover photograph by Tony Tomsic

SCHOLASTIC BOOK SERVICES
NEW YORK • TORONTO • LONDON • AUCKLAND • SYDNEY • TOKYO

Other books by Joel H. Cohen
available through Scholastic Book Services:

Big A: The Story of Lew Alcindor
Cool Cos: The Story of Bill Cosby
Hammerin' Hank of the Braves

1st printing .... November 1971

Contents

1

Last Minute Magic

THE CLOCK and the scoreboard told the hard news: The Houston Oilers were leading the Baltimore Colts by three points with only forty-six seconds left to play in the game.

Johnny Unitas, the Colts' great quarterback — so cool in the clutch people say he has ice water in his veins — had been in tight spots like this before. And often just a sweep of his golden arm had supplied the magic needed for a come-from-behind victory in the closing seconds of play.

Could Johnny again pull off his magic trick on this Sunday afternoon of October 11, 1970?

Unitas took the snap from center, backpedaled, and let go with a pass to the Colts' wide receiver, Roy Jefferson.

As John Idzik, a Baltimore backfield coach, described it to a reporter: "Unitas threw the ball and never watched it go into the end zone. He just turned and walked to the sideline . . . like he knew it would happen."

It did. Jefferson grabbed the pigskin for a touchdown and a 24-20 Colts' win.

Characteristically, Unitas shrugged off his unconcern, saying, "Jefferson had his man beat. There was no reason to believe he wasn't going to catch it."

Jefferson's catch gave the Colts their third victory against one loss. And it was typical of the breath-taking, seesaw way that games often went for the Colts.

It was typical, too, of Johnny Unitas' calm confidence and efficiency. This coolness has marked the brilliant career of the thirty-eight-year-old miracle man whom many consider the greatest quarterback ever.

In his fifteen-year pro career, Johnny Unitas has thrown more passes for more completions, more yardage, and more touchdowns than any other player in the history of professional football.

The Associated Press named him Pro Football Player of the Decade for the 1960's; sportswriters in a Pro Football Hall of Fame poll proclaimed him the Greatest Pro Quarterback of All Time; and fans would vote him the NFL Man of the Year in 1970.

This is all the more remarkable since Johnny has been considered finished so many times. His age combined with an assortment of injuries that would keep "Marcus Welby" and the doctors in "Medical Center" busy for a season have caused many sports fans to count him out more times than a glass-jawed prize fighter.

But time and time again, he's come back strong, flashing his old brilliance and leading the Colts to one stirring victory after another.

The 1970 season was no exception. Fans had heated arguments over Johnny: Was he still the golden-armed, steel-nerved quarterback of old? Or had injuries and time caught up with him?

It was a fair debate. At times during the 1970 season there were indications that he might have lost his touch. But many more instances showed that when the chips were down, no one was better than Johnny U.

2

Hard Knocks:

On and Off the Gridiron

QUIET, good-natured, and wild about ball-playing. That's the way Johnny Unitas is now, and that's the way he was as a boy.

Johnny says: "I guess I was kind of shy and a little backward. I had my own friends and I didn't go out of my way to make myself known. Just sort of brought up the rear of any place I was going. I wasn't much of a talker. In fact, my mother always said getting a sentence out of me was like pulling teeth."

Johnny, the third of four children of Francis and Helen Unitas, was born May 7, 1933, in Brookline, a section of Pittsburgh, Pennsylvania. He began life as a rather husky baby, weighing in at eight pounds, ten ounces. But during his childhood he was always underweight for his height. His mother says that he ate more than anybody else in the family, especially on Thanksgiving Day when "he never got up from the table."

Johnny had many friends, his kid sister Shirley remembers, but he still spent a good deal of time by himself, and "talked only when he absolutely had to."

"Though," his mother says, "he was never scrappy and generally so quiet you never knew he was around," sometimes he had to be punished just like any other boy.

"I got a slap occasionally," Johnny admits, "but that was only if I was being smart alecky or fighting with my sisters. I don't think I was really a bad kid."

His two sisters are inclined to agree. Shirley, who is married to a former high school teammate of Johnny's, confesses that she teased her brother a lot. It used to aggravate her that she couldn't "get a rise" out of him. But, she says, he was always ready to defend her when her tomboyish antics got her into scrapes.

His older sister, Millicent, remembers John's dry sense of humor and his own quiet way of teasing.

Johnny was baptized by his mother's brother, a Roman Catholic priest, and from that uncle he got his middle name, Constantine.

As a small boy, Johnny claims that he had no heroes, sports or otherwise; but there *was* someone he loved: Popeye, the comic strip, radio, and movie character. His grandfather often called him Popeye, and would try to persuade the boy to sing "Popeye the Sailor Man" for the family before dinner.

As a young boy, Johnny was very close to his father, a tall man of Lithuanian background who ran a coal-delivery business. Each evening Johnny and Shirley would rush to the corner to meet his truck. Their father would lift them up into the cab so that they could ride the half block home with him. One evening, though, Johnny was fooling with the door handle, and the door sprang open. He fell out, and the truck came within inches of running over him.

In 1938, when Johnny was only five years old, his father died of pneumonia. It was a terrible loss for the whole family, and especially for Johnny. There were times when the young boy could hardly hold back his tears. But he was learning to do what Shirley said he soon mastered: To "weather everything thrown at him."

When Johnny's father died in the late thirties, America was still struggling out of an economic depression. Some of Mrs. Unitas' well-meaning relatives were afraid that she wouldn't be able to manage for herself and her four youngsters. They suggested that she give the children to someone else to bring up. But she was determined to keep her family together at all cost.

"They're my responsibility and I'll raise them," she said. And raise them she did, even though it meant a great deal of sacrifice and hard work for her.

Unquestionably, Mrs. Unitas' courage in the face of difficulties was a tremendous influence on all her children. Her strong character gave Johnny an example in determination and spirit that has stood him well. His mother never allowed herself to become discouraged and Johnny has shown the same trait in his professional career.

"Our house was clean, and it was mortgaged — just like everybody else's," Johnny explains. "My mother did as well as she possibly could under the circumstances. We always had enough food and we always had clothes on our back."

For a while Mrs. Unitas kept her husband's coal business going, taking orders over the phone and hiring men to drive the delivery truck. When Johnny's brother, Leonard, was old enough, he drove the coal truck, and sometimes Johnny would lend a hand by shoveling the coal on the sidewalk into the basements.

Mrs. Unitas also worked at night, sweeping, dusting, and emptying wastebaskets in an office building.

"She's a very strong person as far as hard work and understanding are concerned," says Johnny. "She worked daytime, nighttime, and did everything she possibly could to take care of us. She even went to night school to get her high school degree. And she passed the Civil Service examination and later became a bookkeeper for the city of Pittsburgh."

During the day, Millicent would help her mother by preparing lunch for her younger brother and sister. And there was always someone to look after them while their mother worked.

Like most children, Johnny and his brother and sisters had chores to do around the house. They took out the garbage, carried out ashes from the furnace, and kept the yard clean and neat. Johnny was in charge of keeping the furnace running all night long. Today you just have to set a thermostat to heat a house. In those days keeping a house heated meant shoveling coal and regulating the damper by hand, and Johnny did it faithfully.

As soon as he was old enough, Johnny worked at odd jobs outside his home to earn money. He washed windows, swept floors, and ran errands.

"He was crazy about animals," says his mother. "He was always bringing home stray cats and dogs."

"My interests," he says of his childhood, "were the same as any boy's: playing ball, going to the movies, reading comic books, shooting marbles. We kids did everything imaginable — there was always something to do." To develop their muscles, Johnny and Leonard would sometimes jab at an old punching bag and lift weights they had made out of old pipes and cement. At times Johnny threw a football through an old tire attached to a swinging rope.

"Like most kids," he says, "I was interested in sports and athletics. Depending on the season, I played basketball, baseball, softball, any sport you could name."

According to his brother, Johnny was very good at baseball and he was a better-than-average basketball player. "He could hold a basketball in one of his meathook hands, and he was so tricky with his passing, half the time his own teammates were fooled."

But Johnny had a particular fondness for football, and luckily, he had more than just fondness for the sport — he had talent and a strong desire to play, and he could absorb a lot of punishment.

In or out of sports, "he never complained, no matter what happened," says his sister Shirley.

Most times, according to Millicent, "you never knew when he was hurt." Even when he had a bad fall and split open an eyebrow, he barely said a word about it.

There were two freak accidents that left their scars on Johnny. The first one happened while he was still in grade school. Johnny and Leonard found an unexploded .38 slug and placed it in the crack of a telephone pole. With a BB gun, they took turns shooting at it. When Leonard suddenly connected, the bullet casing went flying, hitting Johnny in the leg. Some of the fragments are still in his leg.

Years later, Johnny had a second strange accident. He was handling a pistol his mother kept in the house as protection against prowlers. As he held the gun in his left hand, he accidentally pulled the trigger, and a bullet which was still in the weapon went through the index finger on his right hand. Shirley, who happened to be at home when the accident occurred, quickly wrapped up her brother's bleeding finger, and rushed him to a doctor. Despite the splint on the finger of his throwing hand, Johnny went on playing football.

Ever since that accident, Johnny hasn't been able to straighten the first joint of his index finger properly. Sometimes Leonard kids him and tells him that if it hadn't been for the injury, he wouldn't be able to throw straight!

Because he was always getting banged up, his mother tried to discourage him from thinking about football as a career. But Johnny would just smile his lopsided, toothy grin and gently shrug off her concern. Football was what he loved.

One day in grammar school, Johnny's teacher asked her pupils what they wanted to be when they grew up, and the boy unhesitatingly answered: "A professional football player."

He had more confidence in his ability to fulfill that dream than his family did. "He was so thin and fragile, we didn't think he could make it," says Leonard. But Johnny was soon demonstrating that he had the potential to become an excellent ballplayer.

He attended St. Justin's, a Catholic elementary and high school, where he just got by in his school work because he devoted so much time to sports.

In high school, freshmen weren't allowed

to play varsity football, so he had to wait until his sophomore year.

St. Justin's was a small school and could bring together a squad of only about two dozen ballplayers, so Johnny and his teammates had to play both offense and defense. To Johnny it didn't matter what position he played, as long as he played. He started as a halfback and end. Taking over at quarterback on the high school team was just something that developed.

"When our quarterback was hurt a week before the opening game of the season," Johnny vividly recalls, "the coach just threw me in there. He said, 'You're the quarterback; learn the plays.' And that's what I had to do."

Johnny learned the plays and his job so well that he was kept on at quarterback even when the regular player returned and a new coach, Max Carey, took over. Carey believed in Johnny and became a great influence in his life.

"This boy is one of the best passers and T-quarterbacks in Catholic League history," the coach told one newspaper reporter.

Wilbert Rall, coach of a school team that played St. Justin's, was quoted as saying: "Unitas has been a real workhorse for his team and his coach. He has been the back-

Johnny as a high school quarterback. He was outstanding as a passer and team leader.

Johnny with a favorite mutt. He was always bringing home stray cats and dogs.

bone of the St. Justin's ball club with his field generalship, his passing, kicking, running, and defensive play. He's a very quiet and unassuming boy, but he's a package of dynamite on a football field. He's by far one of the finest passers in scholastic football."

There were many qualified observers who agreed with the coach, and in his senior year, Johnny was chosen quarterback on the Pittsburgh All-Catholic High School team. He also won honorable mention on a magazine's All-America high school team.

3

A "No" from Notre Dame

AS A YOUNGSTER, Johnny listened to Notre Dame games on the radio, rooting for the school that has given football such greats as Knute Rockne and the Four Horsemen. Though Johnny was too shy to talk about his daydreams, he must have pictured himself playing first-string quarterback for the Fighting Irish.

"That was the number one school in the country as far as I was concerned and I wanted to be good enough to go there," he says.

Max Carey, Johnny's high school coach, thought he *was* good enough for Notre Dame. He felt John had the arm and the ability and he encouraged him to try for a scholarship.

So the high school sensation, who was now a six-foot-tall beanpole (he weighed only 145 pounds), made the trip to the Notre

Dame campus at South Bend, Indiana. Frank Leahy, then the head football coach at Notre Dame, was out of town, so Bernie Crimmins, a backfield coach, gave Johnny a thorough trial. Crimmins had him work out for a full week, than gave the report to Max Carey: Notre Dame liked the way Johnny played ball, but they felt he was too skinny for them.

"It was a big disappointment," Johnny concedes, "but you have those things in a lifetime. You get knocked down, you've got to get back up."

He got back up by trying out for another college. He worked out for the coaches at Indiana University. But after they shook his hand and thanked him for coming, Johnny never heard from them again. The college world wasn't exactly fighting over the lanky kid from St. Justin's. But Johnny did not give up easily.

Since he lived in the Pittsburgh area, Johnny felt the University of Pittsburgh would be a natural place for him to try next. He applied for admission and worked out at the University one day. He did well on the field but he made a poor showing on the school's entrance examination and wasn't admitted.

Johnny was beginning to feel discouraged.

Then Max Carey, while attending a coaches' clinic, got into a friendly conversation with John Dromo, who was one of the assistant basketball coaches at the University of Louisville in Kentucky. Dromo told Carey that the Louisville Cardinals had the makings of a good football team if only they could acquire a passer. Coach Carey didn't think twice ... he suggested just the person to fill the bill.

Before long Frank Camp, Louisville's head coach, invited Johnny to come to the school for a tryout.

Coach Carey pointed out to John that at Louisville U. he would be a first-stringer rather than a substitute. But Johnny had his heart set on making the pros and he knew that he had less chance of being noticed at Louisville than at a university where the team played top opponents and won nationwide publicity. When no other school showed interest in the lean athlete, though, John went to Louisville for a tryout.

A college entrance examination once again threw him for a loss. It looked as though he would be denied the scholarship he needed if he was ever to attend college. When a summer job was offered to him, he stayed on in Louisville, cleaning up after hours in a tobacco factory.

By August he had convinced the college board of directors how important it was to him to get into college. They consented to let him enter the school on probation. At first he was not permitted to carry a full program of classes but, he says, "I applied myself to the job and showed them I was capable of doing college work. Once they saw that, they took me off probation and I was able to carry as many hours as I wanted."

He majored in physical education, and took courses in economics, social science, and psychology. If he hadn't succeeded as a football player, he probably would have tried teaching and coaching athletics.

He made the varsity team without difficulty, but he was only the third quarterback on the squad. As a freshman, he sat on the bench while the Louisville Cardinals lost three of their first four games.

The truth was that he was still skinny and gawky. In fact, a coach once mistook him for the waterboy, and twice (though he didn't realize it) he was almost sent home because the coach feared he was so thin he'd get hurt.

But Coach Camp recalls that, "though he didn't weigh very much, Johnny practiced awfully hard. He was consistent in his efforts, and finally convinced me how much he really wanted to play."

Before the next game, the coach, who had been alternating quarterbacks, announced, "I've decided to go with the freshman."

At last Johnny had his chance — as starting quarterback against St. Bonaventure at Olean, New York. His performance during the first half was hardly one to encourage a young man with hopes of playing pro ball. The Bonnies tallied nineteen points, while Louisville failed to score at all.

But Johnny, who insists that "I don't have any doubts about anything I'm going to do," had complete confidence in his own ability to move the ball and the team. In the second half, he showed why. He uncorked eleven completions in a row and Louisville surged forward with three touchdowns and a 21-19 lead. Though St. Bonaventure finally won the game with a late field goal, 22-21, Johnny had played well enough to get a hammerlock on the starting quarterback position.

When Johnny is asked about the eleven straight pass completions, he says, "I don't keep track of things like that. The only thing that interests me is whether or not we get enough points to win."

Unfortunately, at Louisville winning

didn't happen very often. "Mostly, I was running for my life," Johnny recalls with a laugh. At that point though, Louisville did manage to follow its close loss to the Bonnies with five victories in a row.

One game stood out especially for the way it established Unitas as the undisputed leader of his team. It was during the first half of a game against heavily favored Houston. Louisville had tied the score at seven-apiece on an interception. Then, with John connecting on eight of nine aerials, the team moved eighty-five yards to lead 14-7 at the half. A fumble recovered by Louisville made it 21-7. Houston kept fighting and early in the fourth quarter knotted the score again.

Late in the fourth quarter, Johnny had moved his team to Houston's 40-yard line. It was fourth down and two yards to go for a first down. Unitas, not wanting to lose possession, planned a pass play, but in the huddle a veteran fullback said, "Give the ball to me; I'll get the two yards." The freshman quarterback snapped back, "When I want you to take it, I'll let you know." Then he called the pass, and with Houston expecting a running play, Johnny threw to end Dave Rivenbach for the touchdown.

Johnny's authority was never questioned after that. Looking back on it, Johnny remarks, "That fullback wanted to test my authority out on the field. Either the quarterback takes charge, or someone else runs the show. I'm sure most people think that the quarterback is always in charge."

"From the outset," coach Frank Camp says, "Johnny was cool and showed a lot of poise. He had a strong arm, knew football, and constantly studied the game. If he had a fault, it was that he wanted to throw too hard." Johnny, who, the coach says, was "real eager to learn," soon learned when to throw hard and when to throw soft.

According to Johnny, Coach Camp's knowledge of the passing game was "just fantastic."

Johnny's freshman year was the only winning season he enjoyed at college because Louisville was de-emphasizing football, and fewer athletes could attend the school on scholarships.

In his sophomore year, the team managed only three victories in eight games, despite the leadership of its talented and determined quarterback. During one game, that ended in a 41-14 win over Florida State, everything seemed to be working. When he saw opposing players converging on him, Johnny even chalked up a fifteen-yard gain by throwing a shovel pass between his legs to an eligible teammate!

Johnny didn't like losing games any more than anyone else did, and — with a pro football career ever in mind — he "always put forth his best effort," his coach says. As poorly as the team was doing, Johnny's performance was excellent.

One of the people who took special notice of Johnny was Bernie Crimmins, who had become head coach at Indiana University. Crimmins, you'll remember, had given Johnny his tryout at Notre Dame and turned him down because he was so skinny.

Now the coach invited Johnny to consider switching to Indiana, a Big Ten school, where there was greater emphasis on football; the competition was keener; and games were played in the national spotlight. Two years earlier Johnny would have jumped at such a tempting offer. Now people were telling him that he would be foolish to let this opportunity pass.

But whether he would make the switch or not, Johnny was determined to go about it in the right way. He felt it was only fair to discuss his decision with those who were closest to him: his mother, his brother, and his high school coach. They had the same feeling that Johnny had.

"When I was looking for a place to go, none of these people wanted me. But Coach Camp took me in and sort of built the team around my throwing ability. It didn't seem fair of me to walk out on him after he had taken me in and given me a full scholarship. So my decision was to stay at Louisville and do everything I could to repay Coach Camp for his confidence and the things that he had done for me."

"This decision — to stick with his first obligation — made me think a great deal of him," says Coach Camp. "I knew he was a great boy."

Sometimes Johnny's way of "repaying" his coach gave the Cardinal rooters heart failure. Unitas dared to throw passes from just in front of his own goal line — and the dangerous surprise often worked, frequently for long gains. These calculated risks convinced his coach, a man who was also willing to take chances to win, that Johnny was "a real competitor."

"I knew what I was doing," says Johnny, the master of gridiron surprise. "I was confident that I could get the ball where I wanted it, if our receivers got open."

Then he adds: "That's all it is, just a matter of having confidence in yourself and trusting in your teammates to do their job while you're trying to execute yours."

During Johnny's junior and senior years, an important football rule was in effect. College teams could no longer make unlimited substitutions, so players stayed in to play both offense and defense. In one rout that Louisville suffered, Johnny played safety and made 85 per cent of the tackles.

During a preseason scrimmage in his senior year, Johnny was hit from behind and suffered a hairline fracture of the ankle. It looked as though the injury might keep him out for the season. He missed the opener, then told his coach he thought he'd be able to play if the ankle was well taped. Johnny on one good ankle was better than most quarterbacks on two, so the coach agreed. Johnny played out the year, learning how to dodge approaching tacklers, how to get passes away at the last possible instant — and, because of his bad ankle, how to throw off-balance. If he wasn't winning games, he was at least acquiring a winning technique.

During his senior year "he couldn't do anything but hobble back and pass," Coach Camp remembers, "but that he did in grand style."

During that same year football scholarships once again became available at Louisville and the team acquired nine new freshmen. But the addition of new players wasn't enough to save the Cardinals from another losing year.

In the four seasons that Unitas played football at the University of Louisville, the Cardinals won only twelve games and lost twenty-two. Still Johnny was able to complete 245 passes in 502 attempts for 27 touchdowns. He set fifteen school records in such categories as "most passes attempted and completed," "most touchdown passes," and "most yardage gained." Many of his records have since been surpassed, but as of 1971 he still holds the school's record for most touchdown passes in a career (twenty-seven). And his record for most touchdown passes in a single game (four) has been tied — but not surpassed.

Unitas never regretted his decision to stay. "I had four good years at Louisville as far as I was concerned," he says. "I met a lot of nice people, got a good education, which is the reason for going to school in the first place, and I played good football. Our team did the best it could against the teams it played. That's all you can ask of anybody."

4

From Steeler to Colt

WHEN HE was graduated from the University of Louisville in 1955, Johnny Unitas carried 190 pounds on his work-toughened six-foot, one-inch frame — enough weight to qualify for the pros. He'd done it by concentrated eating, working and playing hard, and getting enough sleep. By the time he left Louisville, he had won the support of a number of people who believed he had not only the build but the talent to succeed in professional ball.

Johnny had married while he was in college and he and his wife, Dorothy, were the parents of a baby girl. John had to make a living for his family, and he still wanted to make it in pro football.

When his hometown team, the NFL's Pittsburgh Steelers, picked him in the ninth round of the 1955 draft, Unitas was hopeful that he might at least make the squad as substitute signal-caller. He reported to the Steelers' training camp at Olean, New York — the same field where he had started as quarterback in his first college game. But this time, he didn't get a chance to show what he could do.

"The thing grim about it," he recalls now, "was that the Steelers never gave me the opportunity to play."

In scrimmages, he got into only about thirty plays. Though he was in camp through the entire training season, he never got a chance to prove himself, not even in an exhibition game. To keep active he sometimes played catch with the sons of the team owner. These two boys and a wire service photographer, who took a picture of Johnny showing a Chinese nun how to hold a football, seemed to be the only people who noticed him.

At the end of the training season — when it was too late to join another pro team — he was cut from the squad. The Steelers' coach simply explained that the team had too many quarterbacks. Johnny might not have felt so bad if he had been released because his performance was poor. But to be dropped without a fair chance made him feel miserable.

He took the bus fare the Steelers gave him and set out for home in Pittsburgh. By this time, he and his wife were expecting a second child. To save money, he hitchhiked all the sad way home.

Johnny looked for work in Pittsburgh. He helped his brother in the steel-hauling truck business, and took a job laying floor tile for a while. Then he got a better job as a member of a pile-driving crew with a construction gang. One of his duties was to be "highman" or "monkey man," clambering up the rig to grease the chute.

No matter what work he did, football was always on his mind. To keep at the game he joined a semipro eleven, the Bloomfield Rams of the Greater Pittsburgh League. The Rams were coached by Charles (Chuck) Rogers, and they played once a week at the Arsenal Street School playground, a grassless, rocky field that had to be oiled in the summer to keep the dust down.

Since the Rams' season was already under way, Johnny had to sort through a pile of old clothing and equipment to put a uniform together. He started playing on the defensive squad but soon moved over to quarterback.

Writers have often reported that Johnny U. — who would become one of football's highest-paid players — received only six dollars a game for playing with the sandlot team. Johnny says he didn't make even that much. "We got three dollars a game, really. Six dollars was for the *championship* game," he notes, adding with a grin, "because I held out. But it didn't make that much difference. I would have played for nothing."

Playing ball kept Johnny's pro hopes alive. And he looked forward to summer when he would have a tryout with the Cleveland Browns. After the Steelers had released him, Max Carey, his high school coach, had suggested that Johnny send a telegram to the Browns' coach, Paul Brown, saying he was available. It seemed like a good idea for the Browns had shown interest in him when he was in college.

Paul Brown's reply to the telegram said that quarterback, Otto Graham, had come out of retirement, two back-up quarterbacks were still available, and the team did not need another one that season. But he told Johnny he was welcome to come and try out next year.

When word about the Cleveland tryout got around, opposing players sometimes needled Johnny. "Hey Unitas," they would joke, "did you know the Chicago Bears are after me?"

In February 1956, when he was still looking forward to the summer tryout with the Browns, Johnny got a surprise phone call from the Baltimore Colts' general manager, the late Don Kellett. Kellett asked if Johnny was interested in playing for the Colts. When Unitas said yes, Kellett invited him to their camp for a tryout.

Kellett's phone call, which cost the Colts about eighty cents, bought Baltimore an arm worth many times its weight in gold, and a player worth millions. Today teams pay huge bonuses to acquire talented players. The eighty-cent phone call was easily the best bargain in pro football history.

There have been stories that Kellett's interest in Johnny was aroused by a letter from a Unitas fan who suggested that the Colts look at a great quarterback playing for the Bloomfield Rams. The Jets' coach, Weeb Ewbank, then coach of the Colts, still kids Johnny, saying he wrote the letter himself.

But as Johnny tells it, "Mr. Kellett told me he was going through the waiver list to find a back-up quarterback for George Shaw because Gary Kerkorian was going to retire. He came across my name on the list and asked coach Herman Ball, who'd been with the Steelers the year before, about me. Herman said, 'I think the kid can throw the football.' The Colts contacted my college coach and got verification from him, and decided to give me a chance."

Johnny went to Baltimore in the spring, and was invited to training camp that summer. Gone was his dejection over being cut from the Steelers. He was elated about the Colts — and more than elated about his new $7,000 contract.

Johnny — tough and fit from his sandlot football and construction work — quickly demonstrated the power and accuracy of his throwing arm. "That new guy Unitas can *throw*," Fred Schubach, the Colts' equipment manager, remembers telling Kellett, who commented, "I really think this boy is worth a chance."

Johnny got that chance early.

"I was very fortunate," he recalls. "Kerkorian never reported to camp, and another rookie quarterback preferred to play defense rather than take on the responsibilities of pro quarterback." That left George Shaw, the Colts' number one quarterback — and Johnny. When Shaw came down with virus pneumonia, Johnny was elected to play the preseason games.

"I was nervous at first, but I soon got over it," a magazine writer quoted Unitas. "I got smacked around so much, I didn't have time to be nervous. Andy Robustelli busted through and gave me a swipe alongside the head. I must have staggered backward twelve yards.

Then I collected my senses and decided it was discreet to fall down."

Johnny was experiencing the tremendous difference between playing college ball and professional football. "It's altogether different; it's like going back to the first grade," says Unitas, one of the most dedicated students of the game.

According to him, preseason games are especially valuable for the new players. "For the seasoned player," he says, "it's just a matter of getting himself timed up and into playing condition before the season starts. But for the younger player, it's an opportunity to show the coaches just what kind of ability he has.

"There are a lot of players who look good in practice; other players look terrible in practice and altogether different in a ballgame. So you get a two-way look at them, in practice and in the game with pressure on them."

Johnny looked good both ways.

An exhibition against the Steelers — the team that had unceremoniously cut him — was played in Cincinnati. "I had a pretty good night against them," he remembers. "I threw a couple of touchdowns and we went on to beat them. Just showing the Steelers what I was able to do, after not getting an opportunity with them, was a big thrill for me."

A chance meeting in Pittsburgh made his "revenge" seem even sweeter. At a traffic light, his car pulled up alongside another car, carrying Art Rooney, owner of the Steelers; one of his sons; and the late Walt Kiesling, the Steelers' coach. When the boy waved at Johnny, Mr. Rooney asked his son who the man was. "That's the quarterback we tried to tell you about," the boy replied. "The one who beat the Steelers." At the next light, the car caught up to Johnny and Rooney sportingly wished him good luck.

In one preseason game, Johnny played quarterback for both of the Colts' teams. It happened during an intrasquad game the Colts played for the benefit of the police boys' clubs. Johnny would wear the white jersey of one squad until the white team gave up possession of the ball. Then he'd hustle to the sidelines, put on the blue jersey of the other squad, and play with them. He threw touchdowns for both sides. What he liked most about it was that "whichever way it ended up, I was on the winning team."

There were times in practice when Coach Ewbank had his quarterbacks wear red shirts to remind his scrimmaging defensive teammates not to fold, spindle, or mutilate the valuable quarterbacks. But, Johnny comments, "If some guy breaks clean on an offensive guard or tackle, it's kind of hard for him to stop short, and occasionally a guy will rap you.

"I would just as soon have the practice all-out, anyway," he adds, "because then you become accustomed to the contact. You're not standing back there sure that the guy's not going to hit you. You relax and then — boom! — he does. If you know it's live all the way, you're able to protect yourself."

In another intrasquad charity game before the preseason exhibitions with other teams, Johnny quarterbacked one squad and Shaw the other one. The game, played in Baltimore's Memorial Stadium before 38,000 spectators, ended in a 20-20 tie.

In that intrasquad game, Johnny showed how much he had learned from Ewbank's helpful criticisms and suggestions. Unitas completed 14 passes for 288 yards and two touchdowns, scoring one touchdown himself on a quarterback sneak from the one.

Ewbank, impressed with the power and accuracy of Unitas' passes, his size (196 pounds), and his eagerness to learn, told a reporter: "This boy isn't satisfied just to get the long ball down there and hope some-

The Detroit Lions' Sam Williams rushes in to clobber Unitas, who learned early that punishment is part of a passer's life.

body will be able to run fast enough and far enough to get to it. That's what a lot of quarterbacks do. But not Unitas. He waits until his man has a good start downfield, then he measures the target and lets fly with the intention of putting the ball right in the man's hands. It's no accident when he does it. He means to do it, believe me."

In a late preseason match, the Colts met the Philadelphia Eagles in Louisville, and hometown fans had a chance to watch their former college star in action as a pro. He didn't disappoint them. But George Shaw also returned to action in that exhibition, and when the season opened it was Shaw once again calling signals for the Colts.

5

Butterflies and Butterfingers

GEORGE SHAW was the quarterback leading the Colts as they beat the Chicago Bears in the first game of the 1956 season. Games two and three were lost to the Detroit Lions and the Green Bay Packers. In the fourth game, a return match with Chicago, Shaw got his knee torn under a pile-up of ferocious Bears. Suddenly, with the Colts ahead in the second quarter, Unitas was in the game.

"I was a little nervous," he admits. But when asked how long it took him to get rid of the butterflies in his stomach, he replied, "About the first play, I guess."

But Johnny's first performance was far from spectacular. His first pass was intercepted for a touchdown, then he fumbled. There were two more fumbles on hand-offs because the new quarterback and his backfield teammates were not yet familiar with each other's style of play.

In time Unitas would develop into a master at reading defenses, but as a rookie he was inexperienced in that vital quarterbacking skill. He also tried to force the ball to areas he shouldn't have, an invitation to interceptions.

He did throw his first NFL touchdown pass, however, a thirty-six-yarder to end Jim Mutscheller. Otherwise there was little reason to cheer. When the score was tallied, the Bears had whipped the Colts 58-27.

Coach Ewbank tried to console his downhearted rookie. It was hard, he said, for a newcomer to come off the bench in an emergency and immediately play well. But Johnny knew he had to do much better quickly, or he would find himself out as starting quarterback. He was eager for the chance to prove himself; and the Colts, with an injured George Shaw and no third-string quarterback to turn to, had little choice but to give it to him.

Ewbank put Johnny through special practice, running plays with the regular backs and throwing to the prime receivers.

In his second game against Green Bay, Johnny showed he was a quick learner. As a result of his hard work in practice, his hand-offs were better. Two that went to Lenny Moore, who was having an outstanding day, resulted in sensational touchdown runs. Johnny also connected on eight of sixteen passes, two of them for scores. Baltimore won 28-21. For the time at least, Johnny had the job he wanted.

In the next game, against Cleveland, the Browns jumped off to a 7-0 lead. Then, after the Colts recovered a fumble on the Cleveland 35, Johnny went back to pass, but quickly changed his mind. He took off with the ball and made it to the one-yard line. An offside call brought the Colts half a yard closer, and John handed off to Alan "the Horse" Ameche for the score.

In the final quarter it was 7-7 and the Colts were back on their own 27. Unitas guessed that the Browns would be expecting a pass play. So instead, he gave the ball to Lenny Moore, whose fancy brokenfield running carried him all the way to a touchdown and an eventual Colts' 21-7 win.

Johnny's ability to switch gears and surprise his opponents soon won the admiration of other players. Hall of Fame quarterback, Bobby Layne, once jokingly said to Unitas: "I'm going to tell you something that's going to make you a great quarterback."

"What's that?" Johnny asked.

"Just keep running when they think

you're going to throw, and throwing when they think you're going to run."

Layne's "advice" was one of those truths said in jest, and something that Johnny seemed to know intuitively.

"The element of surprise is very important in quarterbacking," says Johnny, "because if you're not able to surprise your opponent, you're typing yourself. You're letting the other team set up the defensive situations and, in effect, call your plays. You don't ever want to get into the position where they can do that to you, because then they've got you.

"You've got to keep the opposing players on their toes, so they don't know whether you're going to throw or run. And when you pass, you must give them no particular idea of where you're going to throw to. Then you've got them off-balance.

"You might call a play that's altogether 'wrong' for that situation. But it works because you've caught your opponents playing the situation," that is, expecting the usual play in a given circumstance, say a pass on the third down with long yardage needed for a first down. "Sure, I'll run the ball occasionally," Johnny adds, "just to show them they can't play the situation. It might be successful; it might not."

Unitas has even deliberately called a play that has little chance of success, in order to shake up the opposition. This bold action has earned him the kind of reputation that any quarterback strives for. Opposing players think, "You never know what he'll do next." Their uncertainty often pays dividends, especially late in the game.

There were times early in his career when Johnny forgot to mix up plays. On the other hand he had to learn not to call the "unpredictable" play so often in a given situation that it became predictable.

He learned well. The win over the Browns was followed by another loss to the Detroit Lions, but in their next game the Colts caught fire for a 56-21 romp over the Los Angeles Rams. Johnny was presented with the game ball by his teammates, who chose him as the game's outstanding player. (There was one odd incident during his first encounter with Detroit: Johnny caught his own pass! "I threw and a defensive lineman tipped the ball. It came directly back to me so I caught it and started running.")

Three losses followed the win over the Los Angeles Rams. Before their final game against the Washington Redskins, the Colts had a 4-7 record.

It looked as though they were going to

lose again. In the last few minutes of the Redskin game, the Colts were down 17-12 when Johnny uncorked a pass from midfield to Jim Mutscheller, racing toward the goal line, and Jim reached for the pigskin at the five. Norb Hecker of the 'Skins deflected it, but Mutscheller lunged backward to snare the ball and, with enemy tacklers clinging to his back, pushed over for a touchdown and a 19-17 victory.

The Colts finished with a 5-7 record for 1956. But the team showed bright promise, especially in the golden arm of its "fill-in" quarterback who had nailed down his job.

During his college career, Unitas had hurled for more than 3,000 yards. During his first year with the pros, Johnny's 110 completions were good for 1,498 yards and nine touchdowns. His 55.6 per cent pass completion mark was the highest ever recorded by an NFL rookie.

In 1957 Johnny developed into one of the most dangerous passers in the league. Hitting his targets with what has been described as "sniper's skill," he drove the Colts to within a hair of the league title. He threw twenty-four touchdown passes, at least one in every game, continuing a string that had started the year before.

Connecting with long and short passes on

46

an excellent 57.1 per cent of his throws, he completed 172 of 301 tosses for a league-leading 2,550 yards. His average of 8.47 yards per pass ranked him third among pro quarterbacks.

He was especially outstanding in two games against the Detroit Lions and their notoriously tough secondary defense. He connected on 30 of 44 attempts for 480 yards and eight touchdowns.

By the first week in December, a winning streak had propelled the Colts to undisputed possession of first place in the Western Conference.

In some games it was Raymond Berry who completed the big play. In other games, it was Alan Ameche, Jim Mutscheller, or Lenny Moore. No matter who the player was, his skill was fused with Johnny Unitas' dazzling play — reading defenses, throwing high, wide, and handsome, and mixing ground plays with unexpected aerials.

In their next game, the Colts met the San Francisco 49ers, who were tied for second place in the Western Conference. Johnny and Lenny Moore collaborated on an eighty-two-yard pass-run touchdown play, the longest of the season. In the same game, Johnny ran up his biggest totals of the year — his highest number of passes (37) and most completions (23) for the most yardage (296). Ironically, these figures weren't enough to take the ballgame. John Brodie, who relieved Y. A. Tittle, threw a fourteen-yard TD with forty-seven seconds left to go, and the 49ers won 17-13.

The loss dropped the Colts into a three-way tie for first place. The following Sunday, they were walloped by the Los Angeles Rams 37-21 and finished a game out of first place.

The Colts were a disappointed team. Yet the season hadn't been that bad. All but one of their losses had been by six points or less. Their 7-5 record of 1957 had given the Colts their first winning season since 1947, the year they acquired their original pro franchise in the All-America Conference. Now they had their highest finish ever since joining the NFL in 1950.

It was the Colts' golden-armed, steel-nerved young quarterback who had made the difference. In 1957, just a year after he had started his pro career, the players of the NFL voted Unitas the "Most Valuable Player."

Johnny was tremendously pleased. He feels that "the awards that mean the most to you are those voted by your own players and the players you play against."

6

No Holding Those Colts

THE COLTS left the gate with a rush in 1958, stampeding the first six opponents they faced.

The season's opener was only a hint of the great things to come, as the brilliant pass-catch combination of Unitas and Raymond Berry clicked for ten completions, 149 yards, and two touchdowns, sparking the team to a 28-15 triumph over the Detroit Lions.

"I throw to the man who gets open the most and the quickest, and Berry just happened to be the one," says John. "I'd say that Raymond has been the best receiver, the most knowledgeable, and the hardest worker, I've ever played with." During his career, Ray Berry caught more passes than any other NFL player, and most of those passes were fired by Johnny U.

In the sixth game of the season, played

in a driving rain, the Colts trampled the Packers for the first shutout that Baltimore had ever recorded, 56-0. But it was a costly victory because Unitas was put out of action during the game with three cracked ribs and a punctured lung. George Shaw filled in handsomely for the hospitalized first-stringer, completing ten of thirteen passes to ice the win.

Unitas was out of action for two games. In the first one, despite competent quarterbacking by Shaw, the New York Giants upset the Colts 24-21. The loss cut Baltimore's conference lead to one game over the Chicago Bears.

But the next week with Shaw still in command, the Colts chalked up a second shutout — this one over the Bears, who took their first whitewashing in 149 games.

The Colts' next contest was at home against the Los Angeles Rams, and Unitas was back in the line-up. The crowd in Baltimore's stadium stirred as the familiar Number 19 came out on the field. Fans couldn't help but wonder: Had the painful injuries and three-week layoff cut Unitas' efficiency?

On the Colts' very first play from scrimmage, Unitas answered the question. He rifled a fifty-eight-yard scoring strike to

Moore! By the game's end, he had also thrown a twelve-yard touchdown pass to Mutscheller, while completing 12 of 18 throws for 218 yards. With a 34-7 win, and their number one quarterback as sharp as ever, the Colts were moving up on the title.

As their tenth game approached, only their loss to the Giants stood between the Colts and an undefeated season. They needed only one victory, plus a loss by the Chicago Bears, to clinch the Western Conference championship.

Of course a championship was just what the capacity crowd in Baltimore's Memorial Stadium was rooting for as the Colts met the San Francisco 49ers.

After the opening kick-off, the 49ers swept 80 yards for a touchdown, and added three more TD's while the Colts managed just one — on a four-yard run by Unitas. At half time, the Colts were down by a lopsided 27-7 score. They didn't look as though they could pull off a championship.

Whatever happened in the locker room at half time, the Colts, led by Unitas, returned to action revived and determined.

Baltimore took the kick-off, and moved sixty-two yards for the touchdown, as Unitas connected on four passes and Ameche plunged over into pay dirt.

At the end of the third quarter, Johnny unloaded a long bomb to Mutscheller, good for fifty yards. Two plays later, in the fourth quarter, Ameche plunged over for his second touchdown. Baltimore fans roared their approval. Now the Colts were really back in the ballgame.

The tenacious Colt defense did its job again, and suddenly it was Baltimore's ball once more.

Lenny Moore broke loose down the sidelines, cut back to the center of the field, and churned straight ahead for a seventy-three-yard touchdown run. Then Steve Myhra came through with his fourth extra point of the day to put the home team ahead 28-27.

The Baltimore fans, shouting hysterically, had even more to cheer about when Unitas clicked with a seven-yard pass to Ray Berry for the final TD of the day. (It was the twenty-third straight game in which Johnny had hurled at least one touchdown pass, and it put him one ahead of Cecil Isbell for the league record in that department.) Myhra's fifth conversion made the final score: Baltimore 35; San Francisco 27.

The Colts had galloped back from a twenty-point lag at half time, scoring twenty-eight points in the second half, twenty-one of them in the last quarter. The

49ers were held scoreless, thanks to five interceptions. It was a remarkable comeback, and the Colts' victory, coupled with a Bears' defeat, clinched the Western Conference title for Baltimore.

"Nobody gave up," Alan Ameche said later, "because John was acting and talking like we were ahead. And pretty soon we *were* ahead."

Unitas' confidence and ability to come through in the clutch were well shown in that final game. The game also was a good illustration of a team's striking a balance between passing and running.

"It's important that you have running," Unitas emphasizes. "One phase of a game sets up another. We like to establish a little bit of a running game so our opponents just can't 'tee off' on our linemen all day long. Otherwise our linemen have to sit and absorb punishment, but with a running attack they can dish out a little bit of it."

The Colts finished out the regular season with two losses which were meaningless since they had already clinched the Western Conference. Unitas and all the Colts had their minds on a more important matter: the NFL championship game against the New York Giants.

7

"The Greatest Game Ever"

FOR MANY FANS the 1958 championship game between the New York Giants and the Baltimore Colts would go down in football history as "the greatest game ever played." Yet the first fifty-eight minutes of play did not seem noteworthy, especially to the Colts, who were on the short end of a 17-14 score.

Then with only two minutes left, the game turned sensational.

The Giants were three points ahead. Short of a first down by a foot, they punted and Baltimore had the ball on its own 14-yard line. The Colts had acres to go, and hardly any time to do it in.

In the huddle, Johnny Unitas, who was strapped into an aluminum corset to protect his injured ribs, declared: "O.K. We've got some eighty yards to go and two minutes to do it in. Now we find out what stuff we're made of."

Four precious seconds were lost on a missed pass to L. G. Dupre. Then Unitas hit Lenny Moore for an eleven-yard gain, missed on another throw, and connected with Ray Berry on a pass play that was good for twenty-five yards. Now there was no more time for huddles; but the Colts knew exactly what they had to do.

Unitas went back to pass and hit Berry again for fifteen more yards. Again Baltimore lined up without a huddle; again a Unitas aerial to Berry clicked; and the third completion in a row to Berry was good for twenty-two yards, to the Giants' 13.

Just seven seconds left to play. Needing three points to tie, Baltimore called on Steve Myhra for a do-or-die field-goal attempt. The ball was snapped and placed on the 20. The Giant line surged forward, trying desperately to block the kick, but Myhra booted the ball over their heads and through the uprights. Tie score!

The fans went wild with excitement. The thrilling, down-to-the-wire, tie game was the signal for the first overtime period ever played in NFL championship history.

According to the rules, a championship game cannot end in a tie. There must be an overtime period. This period is called "sudden death" because as soon as either team scores with anything — a field goal, a touchdown, or a safety — the game is over.

The Giants won the toss and of course elected to receive the kick-off. Steve Myhra kicked off and Don Maynard finally managed to grab the ball and run it back to the 20. After Frank Gifford gained four yards off tackle, Giant quarterback Charlie Conerly missed on a pass attempt. But on the next play he ran for his life and almost — but not quite — got the first down. The Giants, back deep, were forced to give up possession of the ball. They punted and the Colts' safety man Carl Taseff ran it to the 20.

Unitas, a cool, daring field general, calmly put his battle plan to work, interweaving passes with sweeps and plunges, to keep New York off-balance.

He sent L. G. ("Long Gone") Dupre off tackle on an end sweep for a first down. After a long incomplete pass, barely deflected, he faked to Alan Ameche and handed to Dupre, who surged wide for three more yards. Third down and seven to go. A pass could be dangerous, for an interception would probably mean a Giant touchdown. Though any mistake might be fatal, Johnny boldly took his chances. Seeing his primary receiver covered, he threw a dangerous flat pass to Ameche, who was cutting across the 40. Alan speared it and made a first down by inches. After Dupre gained seven on a sweep, Johnny tried another pass but was smeared for a twelve-yard loss. It was third down now and a long fifteen yards to go.

Unitas faded to pass to Moore, but Len was covered by two men. Meanwhile, Berry had faked so well that defensive halfback Carl Karilivacz was flat on his face, leaving Berry an easy, uncovered target. But Unitas didn't throw because Berry wasn't deep enough for a first down. Johnny casually waved to Ray to go deeper. Then he threw a strike to the six-foot, two-inch end's stomach, and Berry made it to the Giant 42.

Johnny called another pass play, but the Giant defenders were expecting it. Dick Modzelewski, who had creamed Unitas before, would surely be eager to do it again, and middle linebacker Sam Huff had been dropping back to help on pass coverage. In a lightning change of plan that is a Unitas trademark, he barked new signals at the line of scrimmage, handed the ball to Ameche, and "the Horse" romped up the middle through Huff's vacated spot for twenty-three yards.

Then it was Berry angling for a Unitas pitch, and taking the ball down to the Giants' eight, in ideal field-goal range. A field goal was expected, but Unitas isn't known for doing the expected. Instead he handed to Ameche for a yard over right guard; then faking another plunge threw a sideline pass to Mutscheller, who grabbed the ball and fell out-of-bounds at the one. The Colts were on the brink of a miracle. On third and goal, Unitas handed off to Ameche who slammed through a wide hole for a touchdown — and a fantastic victory in the first overtime championship ever played!

It was a personal triumph, too. Against a tenacious defense, Unitas, voted the game's MVP, had hit on 26 passes in 40 tries for an NFL play-off record of 349 yards.

Ray Berry had caught twelve of Johnny's passes for 178 yards (both NFL play-off records), and Lenny Moore had grabbed six throws for 101 yards.

For years after the game, fans discussed the shrewd strategy Unitas had used to achieve victory. Much of their interest centered on Johnny's decision to try for the touchdown in the overtime when a field goal would have won the game.

In the locker room after the 23-17 win — there was no try for the extra point after the touchdown — reporters asked Unitas: "Wasn't it too much of a gamble to pass at

Johnny runs the ball in 1958 championship game with Giants. Steel-nerved Unitas led Colts to a breath-taking tie and "sudden death" overtime win.

a time like that when you could have gone for a field goal?"

"Why a gamble?" Johnny replied. "When you know what you're doing, they don't intercept. . . . We were going so good at the end, they couldn't stop us."

In another session with a newsman, he went into a bit more detail. "People still ask me why I didn't go for a field goal. I never thought of it after we got inside the 10-yard line. I selected a short-yardage play because we had good luck with it all season, especially against the Giants."

Jim Lee Howell, the Giants' coach, agreed with the Unitas strategy. "That was smart football," he said. "Not so much risky as just plain smart football. He had our defenders bunched in for the running attack and knew just what he was doing, and he did it very well."

There were other interesting sidelights to that remarkable game. For instance, there was the terse "pep talk" the quiet quarterback gave in the huddle with two minutes to go and the Colts down by three.

"I don't say a lot — just what I feel," he says. "If you're in a tight spot, you make the team aware of it; you say something to them and they have to think to themselves: 'I've got to do a little extra this time.'

"Sometimes I'll say to them: 'Give me another half second, and we'll get six points.'"

Whether his protectors give Unitas that extra half second or not, rivals marvel at how he manages to hold onto the ball right up to the last possible instant.

"You can't intimidate him," Rams' defensive tackle Merlin Olsen once said. "He waits until the last possible second to release the ball, even if it means he's going to take a good licking. When he sees us coming, he knows it's going to hurt, but he just stands there and takes it.

"I think that when he sees you coming, he holds that ball a split second longer than he really needs to — just to let you know he isn't afraid of any man. Then he throws it on the button."

The NFL championship game showed another quality of Unitas that would be underscored many times throughout his career — his brilliance in the last two minutes of play.

"Those last few minutes are something that we work at," he says. The Colts, like other teams, have special drills for handling the closing moments of a game.

"If we're trying to eat up the clock, we run a play, take a long count, make sure nobody goes out-of-bounds, get up slowly from the tackle, and take our time getting back to the huddle.

"If we're trying to save time, we try to move the ball downfield as fast as possible, depending on whether we are trying to get in field-goal range or score a touchdown. We try to do things quicker. We get to the huddle faster. On a run, we get out-of-bounds to stop the clock. We throw sideline passes. I call two or three plays at a time in the huddle so we don't have to huddle every play. We have to be familiar with the different rules and regulations — how to stop the clock and start it."

The Colts usually try to save their time-outs for the last minute or two of the game. "We very rarely take one except then. Even if we're going to get hit with a penalty, I take a time-out," Johnny says.

Asked whether the final minutes give him an extra surge of adrenalin, he replies, "I don't think so. It's just a matter of knowing what you have in your game plan, knowing how to stop the clock or let it go, and keeping your people aware of what you're trying to do. It's not hard."

It wasn't hard for John Unitas. In three short years of pro football, he had brought the Colts to the NFL championship and become football's brightest star.

8

A Master of Deception

IT LOOKED like old times as the NFL champions opened their 1959 season in Baltimore against the Detroit Lions — by the third quarter of the game, the Unitas-Berry combination had connected for a score. It was the twenty-sixth regular-season game in which Johnny had pitched at least one TD, a string he would continue through the season.

The Colts took four of their first five encounters in 1959, then dropped a pair, causing some "experts" to write them off for a second championship.

Then, suddenly the team started a new winning streak. They won three games in a row and captured sole possession of first place by beating the San Francisco 49ers. During the game, Unitas connected on 21 of 36 throws for 273 yards, threw touchdowns to Berry and to Moore, and ran twelve yards himself for a score.

Once again the Colts were within clinching distance of the Western Conference flag.

In the last regularly scheduled game of the season, they took the Rams on in Los Angeles. Early in the game, the Rams shot off to a 10-0 lead and they still held on to a 26-24 edge as the game moved into the final quarter.

With less than five minutes left in the game, the Colts went into action. Johnny passed to Richardson for a TD to put the Colts ahead; Dick Szymanski turned an interception into another score; and Carl Taseff zipped ninety-nine yards with a missed field-goal attempt for Baltimore's final touchdown.

The Colts had triumphed. They had won their second straight Western Conference crown. History had repeated itself in another way: The NFL championship bout would pit them against their "sudden-death" victims of the year before, the New York Giants.

The Colts were considered the most daring team in pro football as they went into the 1959 championship game. It followed. After all, their ace quarterback had acquired a reputation as the coolest, most daring passer in the NFL. Unitas' short, down-and-out passes, his buttonhooks, his *look-ins* (thrown to an end flanker cutting in sharply just be-

yond the line of scrimmage and parallel to it),
and his *slants* (in which the receiver cuts on
an angle for deeper penetration) had propelled Baltimore to its second conference title
in a row.

"Unitas, a gambler, isn't afraid to pass for
short yardage, scorning the laws of average
and common sense," wrote columnist Arthur
Daley in *The New York Times*. As far as
Johnny was concerned, the important thing
was that his gambles paid off.

The Colts were champions. Johnny, who
that season had completed 193 passes for 32
touchdowns, had another NFL record to his
credit. Sportswriters voted Unitas "the professional football player of the year."

In the 1959 championship game, he would
be up against a strong Giant defense, and an
offense directed by Charley Conerly, who
some people thought had the edge on Unitas
in ball handling and faking. Conerly did have
the edge in yards-gained-per-pass, and NFL
players had chosen him as "player of the
year."

The Colts, with a 9-3 season record, were
3½-point favorites over the Giants, who had
finished 10-2. The Giants were bent on
avenging their defeat in the 1958 championship game, and the Colts were equally determined not to let them do it.

The near sellout crowd of 57,545 in Baltimore's Memorial Stadium expected a closely fought contest. They were hoping that the game would provide some of the agonizing excitement of the previous year's sudden-death match.

On the Colts' first series of downs, Unitas, a master of deception, went to work. From his own 41, he faked a hand-off to Ameche. As Ameche hit the line empty-handed, Johnny pumped his arm several times and faked a swing pass to Raymond Berry, who was split wide to the left. Then Unitas faked to halfback Mike Sommers. Meanwhile, Lenny Moore, who had been split wide to the right, sped along the sideline to the Giant 38, picked off Unitas' down-the-middle bullet, faked Lindon Crow out of position, and ran away from Dick Nolan for the score. It was a beautiful fifty-nine-yard play, and Steve Myhra's conversion made the score 7-0. But by half time, two field goals by the Giants' Pat Summerall had cut the Baltimore lead back to a precarious one point.

Summerall booted home a third field goal in the third quarter to give the Giants their first lead (9-7) in what, until then, had been a bitterly fought defensive game. It was

UPI

Giant line charges, as Johnny starts to skirt right end for second-quarter touchdown in 1959 NFL championship game. The Colts won 31-16.

the only time the Colts' opponents would lead that day.

The Giants missed a first down by inches on the Colts' 28. Then early in the fourth quarter the Colts went on an eighty-five-yard rampage that ended with Unitas' five-yard roll out into the end zone, helped by a crunching block by Moore. The extra point made it Baltimore 14; New York 9. The Colts quickly improved their margin. Andy Nelson intercepted a Conerly pass to set up the next Colt TD on a Unitas-to-Richardson toss. A few minutes later, Colt Johnny Sample stole another Conerly pass and sped forty-two yards for another Colt TD. A second Sample theft set up a twenty-five-yard field goal by Myhra. The Colts had marked up a sensational twenty-four points during the final period, while the Giants managed a single TD just thirty-two seconds before the final gun. The score, 31-16, kept the Colts on the top of the football heap.

What had happened? According to the Giants' Sam Huff, "Unitas clobbered us with quickie look-ins and slants. They are the most difficult and dangerous of all pass patterns. But the Colts do them well. What's more, they're impossible to stop."

Jim Lee Howell, the Giants' coach, thought the difference lay in how Unitas "was forever making first downs" on third-down plays. Once he needed seventeen yards on a third down, and passed for twenty-nine; on another third down he needed twenty-one, and he threw for thirty-one.

Unitas, with 18 of 29 passes completed for 264 yards, was for the second year in a row voted the game's outstanding player and was given a new car by *Sport* magazine. In the two championship games, he had 44 pass completions on 69 attempts (a 63.8 percentage), for three touchdowns and 613 yards gained. Ironically, New York had outgained Baltimore by 323 to 280 yards, net rushing and passing in the 1959 encounter. But the statistics that pay off are the final scores. The Colts were still champions.

9

"Mr. Quarterback"
Speaks His Mind

NO ONE appreciates the importance of a quarterback to a team more than "Mr. Quarterback" himself. "He's the man out there directing the attack," Johnny observes, "and if he doesn't do his job right, the team doesn't win ballgames. He's responsible for calling the right plays at the right time.

"If the team is a running team and they don't throw the ball very much, then basically anyone can go in and hand the ball off. If it's a passing team, the quarterback is generally the main cog in the attack."

What qualities does Johnny think a quarterback must have to be great?

"First of all," he says, "a quarterback must be able to throw the football. Then he's got to be able to lead people, make them believe in him. To have them do that, he has to be thorough in his job, know the game, and be able to convince the team that what he's doing is right, even when a play looks like a wrong one. I guess it all adds up to leadership ability.

"Throwing the ball is not that difficult," Johnny continues. "Anybody can go out there and throw. You just need a good strong arm."

What *is* difficult, and what separates the great from the ordinary passer, Johnny willingly concedes, is knowing how, where, and when to throw. "How you throw the ball depends strictly on the defensive man's position on the offensive man. You might have to throw the ball low and away; you might have to throw it high. You might have to throw it behind the receiver." (Unitas has been celebrated for sometimes throwing a pass that makes his receiver double back to catch it. The throw may look like a misfire — actually, it's deliberate.)

Each situation is different and determines how hard Unitas throws the ball. "If you're trying to drive the ball to the receiver, of course you've got to throw harder than you normally do. You throw a long pass, lay it up there, and let him go get it."

Unitas says the bomb is no more difficult to throw than a short pass, and that while a sideline pass has its particular requirements, it's not difficult to throw.

Johnny, who generally throws from a pocket of defenders rather than scrambling or rolling out, hurls with his last two fingers on the laces "just like anybody else does."

The passer's ability to throw while off-balance as offensive tacklers lunge at him is part of the technical skill a quarterback must have. So is a quick release. But Johnny points out, "A quick release is something that's exaggerated a lot. Anybody can get rid of the ball quickly, if he wants to. That's not hard. But a lot of fellows can't get rid of the ball unless they have a whole arm motion. They should be able to just snap the wrist and get rid of it."

According to Johnny an interception is the worst thing that can happen to a passer. How to avoid it? "Try not to force the ball," says Johnny, adding, "Of course, interceptions happen a lot of different ways — a good play by the defensive back, a poor choice by the receiver or quarterback, a poorly run pattern by the receiver, a defensive play by the lineman who hits you as you're throwing the ball. It's not always the quarterback's fault.

"Quarterback position is basic and fundamental, just like every other position in the game of football. There are no secrets about it. It's just the little things that you're able to do that make it seem difficult."

One of the "little things" that Johnny does expertly is use his head "to read defenses and try to beat them." He says "it's just a matter of knowing where the weaknesses are on every defense, and knowing the men you're playing against.

"Once you get to know them, then you know how they're going to play in a certain situation, and you take advantage of it. Everyone has little idiosyncracies."

Sometimes, a minor thing like a defensive man changing the position of his feet alerts Unitas to an approaching change in defensive strategy on which he can capitalize.

"Imagine a certain type of defense, with the opposing team playing man-to-man coverage. Suppose a guy playing defensive secondary has his feet squared up. If I see that he puts that left foot back every time he's going to a zone, that's all I need to know. Before the ball is snapped, I know where I'm going to go with it."

Sometimes a team comes out of the huddle and the quarterback, glancing at the defense's setup, realizes that his planned play is doomed to failure. So at the line of scrimmage he calls the signals for another play.

Plays called at the line of scrimmage —

known as "audibles," "checkoffs," or "automatics" — are dangerous, but they can sometimes change a probable loss into a big gain.

Unitas was particularly good at calling audibles when he felt his strategy should be changed. In recent seasons, however, he hasn't been using them as much because "we're able to dictate the defense simply by running certain offensive formations."

Johnny prefers not to name any of the tough defenders he's faced. "Oh, they've all been tough," he says. "I've been playing an awful long time, and to pick one person over another would be slighting people who I think should get a great deal of consideration, too."

A quarterback has to know as much as he can about the abilities and habits of his opponents. It's essential too that he know his own men; what each man can do and what he can expect of him.

Johnny worked closely with Ray Berry, for example, and the result was their fantastic record of success. Some people consider them the most dynamic pass-catch combination in pro football history.

"We spent an awful lot of time on it," Unitas admits. "We worked at our patterns all the time, so that all Ray would do was tell me which one he was going to run. We had five different ways of running each pattern. We worked, went through them all week long, looked at the films. In those days, we used to get a lot of one-on-one coverage and you could work individually on a man. Raymond would decide how he was going to get open on a certain defender and he'd say, 'This week we're going to use two outside moves — one will be a two-step move; the other will be a five-step move.' He'd label them, 'number one move,' 'number two move.' When he said, 'Two.' Boom! I knew where he'd be."

Ray Berry once commented that, "John had to calculate within a matter of inches how much ground I'd cover at top speed and how high I'd be able to leap. This can be done only with incessant practice."

During a game there's little or no time for discussion in the huddle. As leader, the quarterback usually does the talking. "The only time the men talk is when I ask them a question or there's time-out. They seldom say anything unless I ask."

But on the sidelines or during a time-out, Unitas tries to find out how each man is being played by his defender. For example, a teammate will tell him whether or not he can hook his man inside or run him to the outside. Johnny says of his teammates, "These fellows are the ones who know how they can block their opponents. I can't tell them. They're going to do the job. Suppose a defender is sitting on a man's outside shoulder; it's impossible to take him to the inside. I have to know these things, so I can call the right play and make both his job and mine easier and pick up more yardage."

The Colt's playbook (a "bible" that means a $250 fine if a player loses it) consists of close to three hundred plays with many variations. "But we don't go into a ballgame with all that," Johnny hastens to explain. "We go into a game with ten or twelve passes, ten or twelve runs, depending on the people we're playing against and how they've been able to defense us."

According to Unitas, there is no specific play that gives him more satisfaction than any other. "I enjoy it all. Just being able to gain yardage, score points, regardless of what it is.... Playing football is not that complicated, even though a lot of people, including some coaches, try to make it seem that way."

Even when Johnny is out of the line-up, he is, according to the Colts' present coach Don McCafferty, "always in the ballgame."

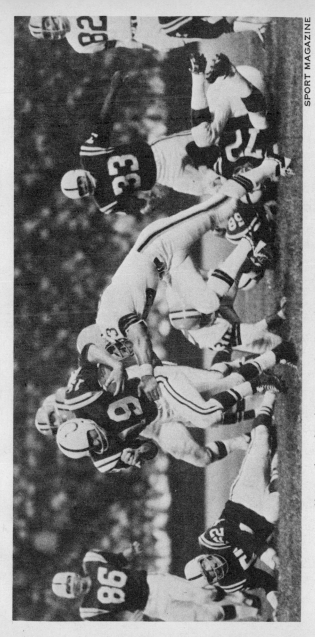

Unitas, shown breaking away for ground gain, would rather run or "eat" the ball than throw it away. He enjoys every phase of the game, even blocking.

Between Unitas and quarterback Earl Morrall, who sometimes replaces him, "there is constant communication on the sidelines."

A different kind of "communication" takes place when the quarterback chews out a receiver who has made a boner.

"I might say something to him," Johnny concedes. "It's more likely I might not. You can't always be perfect throwing a ball; you can't always be perfect catching it. Catching a ball is strictly a matter of concentration on what you're doing. If you continue to drop the ball, you don't stay around too long."

In one game, Johnny threw a perfect pass that would have been a touchdown if a rookie hadn't dropped it. So what did Unitas do? He immediately called the play again, and the rookie not only caught the pass but had his self-confidence restored.

Ask Johnny what statistics — completions, yardage, etc. — indicate a good game personally for a quarterback, and he'll say, "Points are for winners; statistics are for losers. You can beat a team with 401 yards through the air and on the ground, and end up on the short end of the score."

Ask him what constitutes a good game, besides winning, and he'll tell you, "That's *all* that matters."

10

End of a Streak

THE COLTS opened their 1960 season like champions with a 20-0 whitewash of the Washington Redskins. And the one TD pass Unitas threw extended his aerial streak to thirty-eight consecutive games.

The following week, he connected on *four* TD passes as the Colts whipped the Chicago Bears 42-7. It was the fifth time since his streak began that Johnny had connected on four passes for touchdowns in a single game.

Later that season he performed the same magic on successive Sundays in a rout of Dallas 45-7 and in a win over Green Bay 38-24. In the two games, he had connected on 28 of 45 passes for 594 yards. His TD passing streak had moved up to forty-four games.

It looked as if he could go on forever. And go on he did the next week in a second game against Chicago. Despite his second quarter TD pass to Moore, the Colts trailed the Bears 20-17 in the final seconds of the game. By this time, Unitas was groggy and bleeding after being smashed to the ground by an opposing lineman. But he still managed one final pass — and connected with Moore for a touchdown and a 24-20 victory.

The week after that, he hurled three TDs against San Francisco, but the 49ers intercepted five times and beat the Colts 30-22.

Interceptions were still a problem on the following Sunday against Detroit. Johnny threw three of them and the Lions, helped by four fumbles, roared to a 20-15 win at the final gun. But the defeat hadn't stopped Johnny from throwing a pair of touchdown passes, to extend his amazing streak to forty-seven in regular season competition (not counting his TD passes in the two NFL championship games).

On December 11, 1960, the Colts — staggered by two heartbreaking defeats and injuries to key personnel — traveled to Los Angeles, where Johnny's touchdown streak had begun four years earlier, almost to the day.

Through most of the game, the Colts struggled valiantly against the superior defense of the Rams. Deep into the fourth quarter, Unitas had not passed for a touchdown, nor had the Colts scored one. With just ninety seconds left in the game, the Colts trailed 10-3, and Baltimore had the ball on the Rams' 12-yard line. It was a fourth down when Unitas, with one chance left, called for a pass to his key receiver, Ray Berry.

The plan was for Berry to fake to the middle, then break for the right corner of the end zone. The play was called and everything went as planned. Unitas raised his arm and threw the ball to the exact spot; Berry cut, beat his man, then suddenly — fell flat on the ground!

There was nothing Berry could do. One leg was shorter than the other and it had simply given out. Instead of gathering in the tying TD pass, he lay on the ground, pounding it with his fist in his frustration.

So Johnny's streak was over. But his achievement was remarkable, one that compared with Joe DiMaggio's record of at least one hit in fifty-six straight baseball games.

Johnny's mark of forty-seven consecutive games will probably remain unchallenged in the record books for a very long time. Frank Ryan (retired) of Cleveland and Sonny Jurgensen of Washington, his closest challengers, both have only twenty-three.

When Unitas was asked how he felt during the streak, he replied, "I never thought about it. My job was to get out and win the games. If we don't win, I'm disappointed that I didn't perform the way I should."

In the final game of the 1960 season, Johnny was back on the TD pass trail, but the Colts lost again to finish with a disappointing 6-6 season record.

From 1960 through 1970, the Colts amassed the best won-lost record of any NFL team. But through much of the 1960's, Baltimore's fortunes bounced up and down like an elevator out of control. There were many reasons for the team's irregular performance.

Time and wear had taken their toll of a number of old Colts' stars. Alan Ameche had retired and injuries to other players left the Colts without a strong running game to balance their attack. At different times serious injuries sidelined Berry, Mutscheller, and Moore, further crippling the effectiveness of the team.

By the late 60's, some of Baltimore's best receivers, runners, and its great defensive end Gino Marchetti had retired. While the Colts were developing new players to replace those they had lost, the Green Bay Packers were establishing a seemingly unstoppable ball club. Bart Starr's field generalship and passing, the running of Paul Hornung and Jim Taylor, and the hard-driving inspiration of coach Vincent Lombardi had put the Packers in front.

In the early 60's, Unitas was jinxed by injuries. During one of the first games in the 1961 season he jammed the middle finger of his throwing hand, and it stayed swollen and painful throughout the year. His injured finger wasn't the only thing that hurt the Colts; they were handicapped by Ray Berry's preseason knee operation. Baltimore ended the year with an 8-6 record and finished a half game out of second place.

Johnny's injured finger was no longer a problem in 1962, but the team and Johnny were having a bad time. In one game, the Bears gave the Colts the worst beating they had ever had, 57-0. There was a turn for the better, though, in the last two contests of the season. Baltimore and Unitas sparkled with big passing yardage, gigantic fourth-quarter explosions, and two resounding victories. The team had only a 7-7 season, but its strong finish made the Colts feel optimistic about their chances for next year.

At the start of the 1963 season, the team had a new coach, Don Shula. They also had some old problems — injuries and fumbles. In the second game, Ray Berry dislocated his shoulder and was sidelined for five weeks.

The Colts were playing under .500 ball, and seemed headed for defeat by the Minnesota Vikings in their tenth game of the season. With only 3:18 left to play, Baltimore trailed 34-23. Unitas was accustomed to coming through with a late, game-winning score, but this time the Colts needed *two* touchdowns, a near-hopeless situation, even for a miracle man.

But Johnny, without equal in the closing minutes, wasn't giving up. He fired sixty yards to Jimmy Orr for one TD, and the extra point cut the lead to 34-30. Though the Vikings were still on top, the Colts were still alive. But when the Colts got possession again, they had the ball on their own 12, and precious little time remained. The situation reminded many fans of the 1958 championship game.

Once again, Johnny took charge. In only thirty-eight seconds he engineered a seven-play drive that covered eighty-eight yards. The final play was his eleven-yard flip to Orr for a touchdown. The Colts had fought back to win 37-34.

Baltimore won five of its last six games

and amassed an 8-6 record for a third-place finish. Unitas, confident and hitting his targets with precision accuracy, had established an NFL record by completing 237 passes.

The Colts were in good battle condition for the 1964 season. New players helped build their running attack, Lenny Moore was back after an injury, and Unitas was in top form again. With the team's running attack strengthened, opponents could no longer "tee off" on Unitas.

By the third game the Colts showed their new strength. They slaughtered the Bears 52-0, almost the identical shutout score the Bears had administered to them two years earlier. The trouncing established the Baltimore team as a serious contender for the Western Conference title.

The Colts, who had never won more than nine games in a season, rolled up eleven wins in a row and took the Western Conference title with a 12-2 record.

The Eastern Conference title was won by the Cleveland Browns who would be the Colts' opponents in the championship game.

Two days after Christmas, in wind and bitter cold, a huge crowd squeezed itself into Cleveland's Municipal Stadium. Neither team scored in the first half. Then Frank

Ryan at quarterback and Jimmy Brown at fullback made the Cleveland attack click in the second half. At the same time, all sorts of things went wrong with the Colts — fumbles, interceptions, a dropped key pass, and a bobbled snapback from center on a field-goal try. The Browns outran and outpassed the Colts and controlled the game, giving Baltimore a humiliating 27-0 defeat.

The dream of a championship had turned into a nightmare but for Johnny Unitas there were personal honors. He was named the NFL's Most Valuable Player for the second time, and he was an All-Pro choice for the fourth time. He was picked for his eighth Pro Bowl game in as many years; in three of these games, he was elected Most Valuable Player.

11

Pain and Pride

"QUARTERBACKS can't permit themselves to think about injury, or they'll leave their game in the locker room," says Johnny, who has had, among other injuries, a broken vertebra, gashed nose, broken ribs, and a punctured lung. "Quarterbacks have to learn to ignore minor hurts and sometimes even major ones.

"Once a game starts, a good athlete will tend to forget what's bothering him and concentrate on doing the job even though the pain is always there. You just lift yourself a notch or two above it."

The 1965 season gave Johnny several opportunities to do just·that. Except for a 20-17 loss to the Packers in the second game of the season, the Colts were moving right along, trampling every team in their path.

As the Colts moved to Chicago to tangle with the formidable Bears, Baltimore had a

6-1 record, thanks in great measure to Johnny's ability to come through with touchdown aerial strikes in the last minutes of play. The Colts won the game against Chicago but lost their quarterback in the third period. An injured back forced him out of the rest of the game and he missed the next one entirely. But he returned to lead a hard-earned win over the Eagles and a catch-up tie with the Lions.

Next on the Colts' schedule was a rematch with the Bears and their tiger-like defense that had been responsible for Johnny's injured back. This time, with less than five minutes to go in the first half, a couple of Bear tacklers scissored Unitas and he was helped from the field with a severely damaged right knee. He needed an operation and was finished for the season.

Gary Cuozzo, the sub quarterback who took over for Unitas, was himself knocked out of action later in the season and Coach Shula turned to halfback Tom Matte for the quarterback chores. He came through splendidly in the last game of the regular season, and the Colts won to gain a tie with Green Bay for first place in the NFL Western Conference.

The undermanned, gutsy Colts seemed headed for a miracle. With 1:58 to go in the play-off with the Packers, Baltimore led 10-7. Then Packer Don Chandler booted a field goal to send the contest into a "sudden-death" overtime. At 13:39 of the extra period, Chandler did it again for a 13-10 Packer victory. The Colts consoled themselves by winning the Play-Off Bowl for runners-up.

Though he's been injured quite often, Johnny denies that he's ever been the victim of dirty play. "I don't think anything's ever been intentional," he says, adding, "You get hurt. You can't worry about it. If you break a bone, it'll heal. That's part of the game."

There was talk about special rules to protect quarterbacks, especially after Unitas' knee was hurt in 1965. "We don't need any more legislation," Johnny told a sportswriter. "The NFL added another official whose only job, it seems to me, is to protect the quarterback. He stands behind him and when the play is over the official yells at the defense to remind them to lay off the quarterback. From way down under the pile, I can hear that official yelling."

But Johnny says he has no gripes about the officials. "They've got a job to do. I don't think they call everything right. But of course, I don't see everything right, either."

Johnny hurls over the outstretched arm of the Green Bay
Packers' Willie Davis. Unitas, who is known for his coolness
under attack, waits until the last possible moment to pass.

Unitas doesn't get knocked down *every* time he passes, but it happens "quite a bit. It's after the ball is thrown. I'll generally wait until the last second to throw to give my men a little more time to get open. When you do that, you're bound to get rapped. You're going to get hit and get your share of being knocked down. You have to go into the game with that idea — that you may get hit every play."

In 1966 the Colts won six of their first eight games as a result of rugged defense, solid running, and Unitas' on-target aerials. One pass to John Mackey covered eighty-nine yards, the longest pass play in Colt history. The team's two losses were due to fumbles and interceptions.

Baltimore was now tied with Green Bay for first place. The Colts won their seventh game against the surprisingly tough Atlanta Falcons but Unitas hurt his right shoulder during the game.

The rest of the season was a seesaw for Unitas. Some games were won on a last-minute pass. Other games were lost on interceptions or fumbles, or both. But in the season finale, Johnny and the Colts moved back up, defeating the San Francisco 49ers 30-14. Unitas connected on 20 of 30 passes for 339 yards and four scores.

The Colts finished second in the Western Conference, then went on to take their second successive Play-Off Bowl — in the closing moments of the game.

Though shoulder miseries had plagued Unitas through the latter part of the 1966 season, and his performance had been erratic, he smashed league career records for most touchdown passes (232) and yards gained passing (29,593).

When the 1967 season rolled around, Unitas was healthy again, and the Colts looked forward to a very successful season.

The NFL, in the meantime, had been realigned. It was still divided into the Western Conference and the Eastern Conference, but now each Conference had two divisions. Baltimore was assigned to the newly created Coastal Division of the Western Conference.

The Colts started out in spectacular fashion against the Atlanta Falcons. On Baltimore's first play, Unitas fired down the middle to Tom Matte for an eighty-eight-yard score. By half time, the Colts had built a 31-7 lead and they finally won the game 38-31. For the first time in his career, Unitas passed for more than four hundred yards (401). This was one of the twenty-five games in which he has passed for more than three hundred yards, an NFL record.

In the next game, Unitas masterminded a strong win over the Philadelphia Eagles despite a painful "tennis elbow." His right arm, which hurt constantly, felt as though it was being jabbed by a needle whenever he had to snap off a hard throw. Only Johnny and some of his teammates knew how much it hurt him to pass. "I can take an awful lot of pain without it bothering me," he says.

Two more Baltimore victories were followed by two successive ties and another win.

Next on the schedule were the Packers, who had beaten the Colts in five meetings in a row in previous seasons. Green Bay seemed about to hand the Colts their first setback of 1967. With just over two minutes left in the game, the Packers' 10-0 lead looked unbeatable. Then Unitas whipped a TD pass to Alex Hawkins to cut the lead to 10-6. Lou Michaels missed the extra point (meaning the Colts needed more than a field goal), but he executed a perfect on-side kick that rookie Rick Volk recovered for Baltimore. Unitas missed on two passes, but ran for a first down and then, with 1:28 left to play, tossed the game-ending touchdown pass to Willie Richardson for a 13-10 win. The Packers' grip over the Colts had at last been broken.

The Colts then rolled over the Atlanta Falcons, with Unitas connecting on 17 of 20 passes — including twelve completions in a row! — for 370 yards and four touchdowns. The victory was followed by four more wins to keep the Colts' undefeated record intact.

There was just one game to go — against the Rams, who were a game behind Baltimore in the Coastal Division. If the Colts could beat Los Angeles, they would have an undefeated season and a division championship. But an undefeated season was not to be. The Rams' front four dumped Unitas seven times as he was trying to pass. And Rams' quarterback Roman Gabriel fired three TDs. The Rams won 34-10, giving both teams an identical season record of 11-1-2. Before 1967 the NFL rules had required a play-off between teams having identical season records. But now the title automatically went to the team that had outscored the other in the contests between them. So the Rams were Coastal Division champions.

"Two teams that are tied at the end of the year should have a play-off," Unitas was quoted. "It's ridiculous to have one team declared the winner just because they scored more points than you."

Unitas, with one of the finest seasons in his career, was voted the league's Most

Valuable Player for the third time. He set new career records for passing attempts (4,097) and completions (2,261), surpassing Y.A. Tittle's marks in both categories. The 3,428 yards gained passing was only fifty-three yards less than his best previous season. He connected on 255 of 436 pass attempts, a 58.5 percentage. He was elected All-Pro for the sixth time, chosen for the Pro Bowl, and finished second to baseball's Carl Yastrzemski as top athlete of 1967.

Before the 1968 season opened, two of the finest players in pro football history — Raymond Berry and Lenny Moore — had hung up their spikes. So had Jim Parker, the Colts' great offensive lineman.

Even with these losses, the Colts were optimistic. Then, on September 7th, in the final preseason game against Dallas, Unitas, twisting to the left to avoid a rush, snapped a pass to his right without a full arm motion and "felt something pop." He had torn a muscle below and on the inside of his right elbow. Johnny stayed in for a few more series of plays, and probably did his arm more damage. On the bench, he was treated with ice packs and sent home.

As the regular 1968 season began, Earl Morrall, who had been obtained in a trade from the New York Giants, had to take over the reins. Throwing a dozen TD passes, he moved Baltimore to five straight victories. Johnny played briefly in the fifth game.

In the sixth game, against Cleveland, Morrall faltered, and Unitas came in for the second half. He could manage only one completion on eleven passes, before he was replaced by Morrall in a losing cause. Some of the fans booed Unitas.

With his arm puffy and discolored, Johnny sat out the next five games. The Colts returned to the victory trail however and didn't leave it for the rest of the regular season.

For the great quarterback it must have been a bitter pill to swallow — to bide his time on the bench while another man ran his team. But Johnny's reaction to his substitute's success, according to Morrall, was "great. He's been nothing but helpful. He's practically lived with me to teach me the Colts' system." More than once, Johnny suggested a play to Earl that resulted in a touchdown.

In the twelfth game of the season, as the Colts romped over the Atlanta Falcons 44-0, Unitas returned to action in the third quarter. He clicked on five of ten tosses for fifty-four yards. Two games later, he showed good form again while playing the second half. If he couldn't throw as well as before his injury, he was still deadly on slant-ins, and his mastery at reading and picking apart a defense was never better.

But the story of the season was Earl Morrall. While a fantastic Baltimore defense held opponents at bay, Earl led the club to victory after victory, including a 24-14 triumph over the Vikings for the Western Conference championship. Then he put the frosting on the cake by a near-perfect 34-0 trouncing of the Eastern Conference winners, the Browns, for the coveted NFL championship.

12

Super Bowl 3

THE COLTS got ready for football's biggest event — the Super Bowl between the NFL champion and the top team in the American Football League.

At one time the NFL champions were considered *world* champions because the American Football League did not exist. But the AFL came into being in 1960, and since the 1966 season, the top NFL club had met the AFL champions to decide the world title.

Two Super Bowl games had been played thus far, and the Green Bay Packers (NFL) had won both easily. Now the 1968 NFL champions, the Colts, were favored to win against the AFL champions, the New York Jets. The Jets were led by their flashy, super-confident quarterback, Joe Namath, the AFL's Most Valuable Player.

Unitas, still hampered by his injured arm, pronounced himself ready to play. But

Coach Shula gave the starting nod to Earl Morrall, the "Super Sub" who had led the team through the season, the man voted the NFL's Most Valuable Player.

The first quarter of the Super Bowl, played in Miami, was scoreless. Then, with Joe Namath's passing and Matt Snell's running, the Jets marched eighty yards for a touchdown to lead 7-0 at the half.

Was an upset in the making? It certainly looked that way, as two field goals by the Jet's Jim Turner made the score 13-0 late in the third quarter.

Suddenly a murmur passed through the stadium. Number 19 was starting to warm up. The Baltimore miracle man, Unitas, had moved from the telephones to a place near the bench, and adjusting his helmet, he began to throw the ball easily to teammates.

When Johnny went in, the huge crowd stood and cheered him in recognition of his greatness and courage.

From the Baltimore 20, Johnny passed short and the ball fell, incomplete. A run gained only a couple of yards, and another pass went out-of-bounds, so the Colts gave up the ball.

The Jets got into field-goal position again, and Turner booted the ball through the uprights for a 16-0 lead.

When the Colts got the ball again, Johnny U. — the only hope remaining between the Colts and a tremendous upset defeat — went back on the field. Two hand-offs and a short pass; soon the Colts were on the New York 25. Was there still another miracle up his sleeve?

Eight minutes to play. A wobbly pass fell short. Then Johnny spotted Orr in the end zone alone, and what should have been a bullet floated and dived and was nabbed by Jets' defensive back, Randy Beverly.

The Jets — and everybody else — thought it was all over.

Then the Colts had the ball again. But on the fourth down, they were way back on their own 20. To give up the ball now would seal their doom. A touchdown, and there'd still be life.

Unitas went back, and, ignoring the charging defenders, threw to Orr at midfield for a first down. Then the clutch quarterback added one first down after another. Finally, on third down, Hill charged over from the one. The score was 16-7. The Colts were still alive thanks to their field general, Johnny Unitas.

Everybody knew the Colts would try an onside kick — they had to. The kick worked perfectly, and the Colts recovered the ball

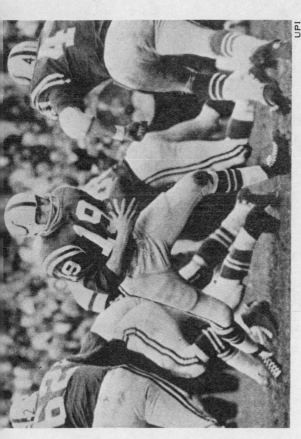

Unitas, out most of 1968 with an injured arm, comes off the bench in Super Bowl 3 to lead a final period TD drive against Jets, but New York won 16-7.

on the Jet 44 with 3:14 to go in the game. Back came Johnny Unitas. He moved the team on three passes in a row to within striking distance. Then, after a missed pair, it was fourth down and five on the Jets' 19; ninety seconds of play remained. Should the Colts go for a field goal or a touchdown? They needed both. Coach Shula decided to try for a TD. Johnny passed, as the Jets surged in. Baltimore fans groaned out loud as the ball fell incomplete.

The Jets had possession, and even the most ardent Colts' rooter knew Baltimore had lost. Johnny had the ball once more, but he couldn't score. It was the first time an NFL team had lost the Super Bowl.

Johnny, who credited Earl Morrall with a "tremendous job" during the '68 season, still maintains the Colts might have won Super Bowl 3 if there had been more time left after Baltimore gained the momentum. He adds with a laugh, "I go back to that old adage Bobby Layne always used: 'I never lost a ballgame yet, the clock just ran out!'"

13

Getting Back in Shape

JOHNNY followed the advice of doctors and trainers and devoted the first half of 1969 to getting his arm back in shape. Five days a week, he went to Kernan's Hospital for Crippled Children in Baltimore for whirlpool baths for his elbow, electric shock treatments, rubdowns, weight-lifting — and throwing. During that time it's possible that he threw more to Bill Neill, the hospital's director of physical therapy, than to any "receiver" since Ray Berry.

Johnny hadn't been able to put speed on the ball during the 1968 season. Now he fired it, although he still felt pain.

By July of 1969, he could tell a reporter, "My arm feels stronger now than before it was hurt. My right arm had fifteen pounds less efficiency than the left, and a fifteen-degree crook in it. Now I can lift just as much weight with the right as I can with the left. I have thrown hard and long, short and soft. Next I go to camp with the rookies. Will I take the quarterback job away from Earl Morrall? I sincerely hope so."

In three exhibition games Johnny showed how far he had come. He played one quarter of a game against the San Diego Chargers and completed seven of eight passes for eighty-six yards. He showed strength and speed and his arm felt fine. He still couldn't extend it fully, but he said he didn't need to.

In the Colts' next outing, he mixed up runs and passes, short and long heaves, to beat the Oakland Raiders, proving that a precision artist doesn't lose his touch.

Unitas had won his job back.

Against the New Orleans Saints early in the 1969 season, Johnny passed for three TDs and 319 yards. Later, he came into a game with the Bears (which Morrall had started) in the fourth quarter. The Bears led 21-14, and, with only 7:40 to go in the game, expected Unitas to throw one pass after another. He didn't disappoint them. He hit on three straight aerials. Then, with defenders prepared for additional passes, he called one running play after another — for a touchdown. The extra point tied the game, and later Lou Michaels' field goal won it 24-21 for the Colts.

The thirty-six-year-old veteran had thrown with his old style and enjoyed a respectable comeback year. He completed 178 of 327 passes for 2,342 yards, but he had thrown more interceptions (20) than TD passes (12).

The Colts had split their first six games of the 1969 season and ended with an 8-5-1 record, good enough for second place in the Coastal Division.

In 1970 the Colts had a new coach. Don McCafferty, who'd been an assistant coach for eleven years, moved up to replace Don Shula, who became head coach of the Miami Dolphins.

During the same year, the American Football League and the National Football League merged into one league, the National Football League (NFL). And the NFL was divided into two *conferences* named the National Football Conference and the American Football Conference, each with three divisions.

The Baltimore Colts, the Cleveland Browns, and the Pittsburgh Steelers — all NFL teams — joined ten former AFL clubs to make up the new American Football Conference. The Colts were placed in the Eastern Division of the American Football Conference, along with the Boston Patriots, Buffalo Bills, Miami Dolphins, and New York Jets.

As far as the pro football expansion is concerned, Johnny says, "Fans still see the same brand of football. There's just as much hitting, blocking, and tackling going on. It's the same game. But spectators just don't see as many outstanding players on one team — the stars — as they did before. Just look at our ball club: Some of the people we have on the club now would have had a hard time making a team like ours was ten years ago."

The Colts and the other NFL teams that were now a part of the new American Football Conference realized that they would have to adjust to the "bump and run" kind of defense the AFL clubs usually played. In the "bump and run defense," defending backs come in to meet potential pass receivers at the line and keep bumping them to slow them up and break their momentum (a tactic that is legal until the ball is in the air).

Unitas found this type of defense of no particular concern. "It's not that much different," he said, "except that the offensive linemen's job might be a little bit harder, because they have to protect a little bit longer than normally." But he added, "There are weaknesses in every defense. You have to find out what your opponent is playing and beat his defense."

In the opening game of the 1970 season, the Colts faced the San Diego Chargers. Late in the game Unitas moved his team within kicking range with only a minute to go and the Colts a point behind. Jim O'Brien emerged as Baltimore's hero as he kicked his third field goal of the game to give the Colts a 16-14 win over the Chargers.

But Baltimore paid a high price for that opening victory. Tom Matte was injured and lost for the season, and Johnny suffered a sprained knee. The knee hampered him in the season's second outing — a Monday night game with Kansas City, which was televised for a huge, nationwide audience.

Johnny played one of the worst games in his fifteen seasons as a pro. He was intercepted three times, completed only five of fifteen passes, and lost a fumble to the Chiefs as their charging linemen swarmed through to smear him time and time again.

Baltimore fans began to boo him. ("They paid their money and they have the right," he said afterward.) Johnny came off the field as Earl Morrall, the Colts' number two signal-caller, replaced him.

Johnny offered no alibis after this humiliating defeat, although he had played with a sprained knee and without the help of his best running back, Matte. Enemy defenders had made the most of Matte's absence. Because the Chiefs didn't have to worry about a strong Baltimore running attack, they had been able to concentrate on decking Unitas.

His performance in the 44-24 trouncing started the whispers again: Had the untiring, courageous quarterback really lost his touch? Had injuries and time finally caught up with him?

The next week end Unitas' skill and know-how answered the questions. Against the Boston Patriots the Colts needed short yardage on a third down late in the fourth quarter. Boston was expecting a power play when Johnny drilled a fifty-five-yard scoring pass to Jefferson for a 14-6 win.

Baltimore's next game was the thrilling victory of October 11 over the Houston Oilers, ending with the last-minute pass Johnny didn't watch being caught. Unitas certainly wasn't playing like a man who was through.

Four victories in a row followed the win over Houston. One contest was a cherished triumph over Joe Namath and the Jets, who had beaten the Colts in Super Bowl 3 at the end of the 1968 season. During the 1970 game with the Jets, Johnny completed his 2,500th career pass. His aerials have gained more than twenty-one *miles* for the Colts.

After the Colts' victory over the Jets 29-22, Baltimore handed a 27-3 beating to the Patriots (Johnny threw three TD's) ; routed the Miami Dolphins 35-0; and trimmed the Packers 13-10. The fans were cheering Johnny Unitas again.

With a team that has won seven out of eight games — as the Colts had — complacency is always a threat. Apparently the Colts did get rather self-satisfied. At any rate, the Buffalo Bills, quarterbacked by Dennis Shaw, held them to a 17-all tie and then the Miami Dolphins took their revenge 34-17.

Next on the agenda were the Chicago Bears, and it looked like another Baltimore loss in the making. Early in the contest, Unitas was hitting the Bears' defensive men more often than his own receivers, and Chicago led 17-0.

But Johnny could still deliver the long bomb when needed, and he showed his talent for quick thinking and decisions. In a play that coach Don McCafferty picks as possibly the big one of the season, Johnny prepared to fire the ball to primary receiver Jimmy Orr. Seeing the Bears' defenders rotate toward Orr, he quickly changed his tactics and launched a rocket to John Mackey who was all alone. The pass was good for a fifty-four-yard touchdown and a 21-20 victory.

"That was the play that got us over the hump," Coach McCafferty said, "and it wasn't tricky. It was actually a broken defensive assignment on the Bears' part. To me, our season then began an upswing."

But Unitas wasn't satisfied with the way the team was performing. With the coach's O.K., he called a players-only meeting. Though the Colts were leading the AFC's Eastern Division by a game-and-a-half, he felt that the team had to talk over some things.

Whatever was said in that Saturday night session must have been magic, because the next afternoon — on a bitterly cold and windy day in Baltimore — the Colts were red-hot.

The Philadelphia Eagles won the toss and elected to kick so that the Colts would have to play into the forty-mile-an-hour wind that was whipping downfield.

"I had never played against a wind that strong," Unitas said later. But he knew what he was going to do about it. "The idea is to throw short stuff because obviously you can't risk anything that will hang up there too long."

He did just that, expertly mixing his pass calls with running plays for Sam Havrilak and Tom Nowatzke with maximum effect.

On one third down and eight, he managed to duck under a charging defensive end and find Roy Jefferson with a pass for a ten-yard gain. Eagles' end Ernie Calloway described what happened afterward. "He gave me an eye fake and raised his arm. I jumped up and tried to block it. He's hip, too. He was never in a hurry."

Johnny led his club to two first-period touchdowns in the Colts' 29-10 triumph over the Eagles, and Baltimore was on its way.

Though the Bills proved tough again, the Colts won 20-14. In the regular-season finale, a rematch with the New York Jets, Earl Morrall took over from Unitas with the Colts behind 7-0 and engineered a 35-20 victory. The Colts finished as the best team in the Eastern Division with eleven victories, two losses, and one tie.

Several teams were in contention for play-off berths under the new league setup.

"It really doesn't make any difference to me who we face in the play-offs," Johnny said. "It's all a matter of preparation and execution, regardless of the opponent."

Against the Cincinnati Bengals, in the AFC divisional play-off, Baltimore's preparation and execution were more than adequate. Sharp Colts' defenders contained the Bengals' runners and bottled up the passing attack. The Colts' running back and blocker, rookie Norm Bulaich, sliced through the Cincy defense as if it were butter. Jim O'Brien booted a forty-four-yard field goal in a shifting wind. And hunched-over Johnny Unitas hurled the pigskin through that treacherous wind for two third-down touchdowns in an easy 17-0 victory. Johnny even broke away for a seventeen-yard run, the biggest ground gain of the day.

But the fault-finders, who maintained that Baltimore's season had been mostly against "losers," predicted that Johnny and the Colts would have tough going against the Oakland Raiders in their second play-off battle for the AFC championship.

But in the game Unitas, cool as always, read the defense and picked it apart. The canny quarterback, who says simply, "You can only do your best," did his best.

In the first period he got his team close enough to paydirt for O'Brien to kick a field goal from the 16-yard line. Later in the same period, he moved the Colts close, and Bulaich slashed off left guard from the two to make it 10-0 with the extra point.

When the Raiders tied the game in the third quarter, Baltimore came back with a field goal by O'Brien. Then Unitas called the old Statue of Liberty play — the kind of play school kids use, where a player holds the ball up as if to pass and another sweeps by and takes it from him. Bulaich took the ball from Unitas at the 11 and ran it to the corner of the end zone. The Colts led again 20-10.

When the Raiders came back within three points, early in the fourth quarter, Unitas took command. On third down and eleven, he passed to Ray Perkins — and got not just a *first* down, but a *touchdown*.

(The Colts had figured the Raiders would play Perkins as tight end and that Orr would come open, but Oakland played it the opposite way. "Unitas read the coverage perfectly," said Coach McCafferty.)

The play, good for sixty-eight yards, was the ballgame 27-17. The Colts, who hadn't fumbled or thrown an interception in their two play-off games, were AFC champions — and headed once again for the most dramatic single event in big-time team sports competition, the Super Bowl.

14
Super Bowl 5

THE SUN was shining in Miami's Orange Bowl on that Sunday afternoon, January 17, 1971, as two teams locked in bone-crunching combat for the NFL championship. The combatants were the Baltimore Colts, winners of the NFL's American Conference, and the Dallas Cowboys, tops in the league's National Conference.

Dallas' "Doomsday Defense" had allowed only one touchdown in their last twenty-five quarters, and the Cowboys were a $2\frac{1}{2}$-3 point favorite to win Super Bowl 5. Not that anyone was conceding them the game!

For one thing, at quarterback for the Colts was the familiar, slightly stoop-shouldered figure of Johnny Unitas. At thirty-seven, this chance-taking wizard of odds — Mr. Cool in the Clutch — was trying for another world championship.

The Cowboys were the first to score, recovering a fumbled punt on the Baltimore nine and calling on Mike Clark for a field goal. Clark repeated his successful kick in the second quarter and Dallas led 6-0.

Then the most controversial play of the afternoon occurred. From the Colt 25, Unitas faded into his pocket of protectors and threw a pass about twenty yards to Eddie Hinton, who leaped to grab the high throw but just managed to get his fingertips on it.

The pigskin grazed a Dallas player's fingertips and landed in the hands of the Colts' tight end, John Mackey, who raced the remaining distance to the end zone.

Mackey held the ball high in triumph, while the Cowboys vehemently protested that the ball had not been touched by one of their own men as it passed from Hinton's fingertips to Mackey's grasp. (A pass is incomplete if two offensive players touch the ball in succession without a defensive player's touching it in between.) But the officials ruled that the ball *had* been touched by a Cowboy — and the touchdown counted. The score stayed tied as Baltimore's try for the extra point was blocked.

When the Colts had possession of the ball again, Dallas linebacker Lee Roy Jordan jarred Unitas into a fumble at the Colt 28.

The fumble set up a Cowboy touchdown on a pass from Dallas quarterback Craig Morton to Duane Thomas. The extra point gave the Cowboys a 13-6 lead.

(Recalling the fumble, Johnny — the NFL record-holder for lifetime fumbles — later commented: "He just knocked the ball out of my arm. He gave me a pretty good shot, but I had no reason to fumble. I should have put my other hand over the ball when I saw him coming.")

Baltimore had something beside the score to worry about. Late in the second quarter as Unitas was set to pass, George Andrie, an expert pass-rusher, broke through and caught him in the ribs with his helmet. The pass was intercepted, but even more damaging, Johnny's bruised ribs forced him to the sidelines. Luckily, no ribs were broken, and Johnny, blessed with an ability to play well even with a lot of pain, felt ready to return to the line-up at any time. It wasn't destined to be.

On the sidelines, Unitas pressed an ice pack to his bruised ribs, while Earl Morrall, his roommate and friend, replaced him, just as Johnny had taken over for Earl in the 1969 Super Bowl loss to the Jets.

As the Dallas-Baltimore game progressed, some people wondered if either team really wanted to be world champion. Fumbles, interceptions, a dropped kick-off — mistakes were committed by both sides.

With eight minutes left, a Dallas pass bounced off Walt Garrison's hands, was tipped by the Colts' Jim Duncan, and picked out of the air by Colt Rick Volk. Rick traveled thirty yards to the Dallas three, and on the second attempt, Tom Nowatzke went over for the TD. O'Brien's extra point tied the score at 13-all.

Now the Cowboys moved into Baltimore territory. On third down and thirty-five, Craig Morton passed to Dan Reeves, who leaped for the catch. The ball bounced off his hands and dropped into the eager arms of Colts' linebacker Mike Curtis, who ran it to the Cowboys' 28. It was the sixth interception of the game, a championship record that both teams would prefer to forget.

With only nine seconds left, the fans in the Orange Bowl and countless millions watching on TV geared themselves for a "sudden-death" overtime period.

Time was called, and in came Jim O'Brien, the rookie place-kicker. The ball was snapped. Eight seconds, seven seconds, six — and with five seconds left — O'Brien booted the ball over frantic Dallas rushers. The ball, hit hard and square, sailed over the crossbar

Johnny and fellow Colt quarterback, Earl Morrall, talk over
strategy for Super Bowl 5 game against Dallas Cowboys. Earl
took over when Johnny was injured and the Colts won 16-13.

between the uprights. It was good for three points and a 16-13 victory to establish the Colts as world champions.

For Johnny Unitas, who had connected on only three of nine passes for eighty-eight yards (including the controversial seventy-five-yard TD play to Mackey), the game was far from a personal triumph. He thought it was a good, hard-hitting defensive game on both sides. But "I was kind of disappointed in what we were able to accomplish offensively, although we scored enough points to win, and that's the main concern," he said several weeks after the game.

Johnny also said that he could have played in the second half, though it would have been painful. He didn't feel good about not returning to action ("But that's the way it is"), yet he was happy for Earl Morrall. "I felt great for him."

Though the two men compete for the same starting position, Johnny says, "We try to help each other whenever we can. The ultimate thing is to win, as far as we're concerned."

In Unitas and Morrall, Coach McCafferty feels his team has "two of the best quarterbacks in professional football." The Colts showed their high regard for Unitas when, part-way through the championship season, they gave him an unusual thirteen-year contract that would keep him with the organization for years after his playing career is over. Their hope was that he would play through the 1973 season.

A few weeks after Super Bowl 5, the Colts' genial head trainer, Ed Block, commented: "Johnny's ribs are still sore, but he doesn't complain. This is supposed to be a tough business, and he lives up to it."

About the same time, Johnny said throwing was no problem for him. "The arm's not as strong as it once used to be, but I can still get the ball down there, sixty yards if need be. No problem throwing it. It's probably a lot easier now because I have the knowledge and know-how of what the other team is going to do, and I know where to go — rather than try to force something, as I might have done earlier. . . ."

As for his health, he reported that he was feeling fine. "I had a few things bothering me this past year but they'll all heal up within the next six months and I'll be ready to go in July." As it turned out, he wasn't.

In early April, while Johnny was playing paddle ball with teammate Tom Matte, he severed the Achilles tendon in his right heel. The very painful injury required an operation. While the surgery was pronounced a success, with healing time an estimated six weeks, only performance on the field would show whether the great Johnny U. could come back again.

Asked whether he thought Johnny could be ready for action when the 1971 season rolled around, John Mackey, the Colts' tight end, told *The Sporting News:* "If anybody can come back that fast, John can. He is an athlete who will pay any price to play football."

Return or not, Unitas had already left an indelible mark in the pages of pro football history, setting records of excellence that are likely to hold up indefinitely.

15

Rate the Great

FAME AND FORTUNE aside, has Johnny Unitas been happy in pro football?

"Well, if I wasn't happy, I would have quit. If you're not happy at what you're doing, you're not giving your best effort."

Johnny is the kind of person who gives his best — off the field as well as on, whether it's visiting servicemen in Vietnam, recruiting for the police department, or helping neglected children.

Among the honors he received for the 1970 season, for example, was the fans' vote as "NFL Man of the Year." The designation was the result of a season-long competition sponsored by Vitalis and supervised by the Pro Football Hall of Fame in Canton, Ohio. The award (which carries a $25,000 scholarship fund in Unitas' name for youth in Baltimore) was not only in recognition of Johnny's over-all playing ability, but his civic involvement — mostly for children.

Johnny Unitas has been known to turn down a high-paying commercial engagement while making a visit to a sick child at his own expense. He has been active in the Big Brother movement, the Crippled Children's Association, the Maryland Special Olympics for Retarded Children, and the Muscular Dystrophy Association, among others. Frequently, he makes unpublicized visits to children's hospitals.

It's an open secret that Johnny has a soft spot for children. "Young people come across a lot more honest than many adults do. They don't try to fool you or give you a lot of backtalk or double-talk. They're going to say what's on their minds."

As to his own children — Janice, 16; John, Jr., 15; Robert, 13; Christopher, 12; and Kenneth, 3 — he wants to see them enjoy themselves and he tries to give them more than he had in his own childhood. But he disciplines them, too. He feels that what his sons and daughter decide to do with their lives is their business. "All you can do is try to help them, try to guide them along the right way. I never try to force them into anything."

If a son of his tried to make pro football his career, it could, he agrees, be a hardship on the youngster because people would tend to compare even the rookie with his veteran pro father.

Johnny sometimes plays ball with his sons. His oldest boy plays quarterback for his high school team. Johnny doesn't give instructions on how he should play, but: "If he wants help, I'll do anything I can for him."

Unitas believes strongly in the importance of sports for youngsters. "You learn so many things from the organized games, things you may never learn strictly from just going to school." He tends to feel, though, that too many young people don't take advantage of sports programs available at school.

Obviously content and at peace with himself, Johnny Unitas was asked whether there is anyone else in the world he'd like to be.

"No, just me," he declares. "Whether I was playing football or not."

Are great quarterbacks born or made?

Unitas says, "To a certain extent, the skills we have are given to us; the matter of whether they're developed or not is strictly up to the individual. You can be anything you want to be, but you have to develop it, work at it. Except for born geniuses, I don't think anything is just natural with anybody."

It's probably not surprising, then, that except for being "bugged" by the squad meetings which he's been through time and again, Johnny even likes training camp. Here for months, players spend long hours working themselves into shape and perfecting their game, excercising, studying, reading, watching films. Quarterbacks run, pass, coordinate plays with offensive backs and linemen. Practice goes on throughout the season.

Always trying to improve his playing, Unitas, after practice, will run certain patterns with receivers and running backs to perfect timing and other essentials.

Asked to name the outstanding quarterbacks now active, Unitas off-handedly names John Brodie, Sonny Jurgensen, Joe Namath, and Bart Starr. "Bart's probably been one of the best quarterbacks throughout the years. He's had good people playing with him, but he does a great job of running an offense and keeping you off-balance. Jurgensen's strictly a thrower. He hasn't had much to run with. Brodie does a good job, gets a lot of good play action stuff because he has pretty good runners. Namath's strictly a thrower. . . . When you talk about quarterbacks, you talk about passers."

He believes Buffalo's Dennis Shaw "is prob-

Unitas takes the snap from center, ready to pass. Rated pro football's greatest quarterback, he's passed for more yards and TDs than any other quarterback in pro history.

ably the best rookie that I've seen come up in a couple of years as far as a thrower is concerned."

Unitas was withholding judgment on Stanford's Jim Plunkett and other untried pro newcomers. He says the fact that "you throw the ball well in college doesn't mean you're necessarily going to throw it well up here."

And what of Unitas? Many consider him the greatest of all.

To coach Don McCafferty, Johnny's greatness lies in a combination of factors. "He's a winner," the coach says, "one of the greatest passers of all time. He's physically and mentally tough. He has a lot of poise and composure.

"He gives the game all he has. He's always fighting. It's the easiest thing in the world to quit. In football, as in life, you have setbacks and every day isn't a happy day. But you don't give up. There are losers and there are winners, even in pro football; Johnny is a winner."

JOHN UNITAS' REGULAR-SEASON RECORD*

YEAR	RUSHING			PASSING					
	Att	Yards	Avg	Att.	Comp	Pct	Yards	Int	TDs
1956	28	155	5.5	198	110	55.6	1,498	10	9
1957	42	171	5.3	301	172	57.1	2,550	17	24
1958	33	139	4.2	263	136	51.7	2,007	7	19
1959	29	145	5.0	367	193	52.6	2,899	14	32
1960	36	195	5.4	378	190	50.3	3,099	24	25
1961	54	190	3.5	420	229	54.5	2,990	24	16
1962	50	137	2.7	389	222	57.1	2,967	23	23
1963	47	224	4.8	410	237	57.8	3,481	12	20
1964	37	162	4.4	305	158	51.8	2,824	6	19
1965	17	68	4.0	282	164	58.2	2,530	12	23
1966	20	44	2.2	348	195	56.0	2,748	24	22
1967	22	87	3.9	436	255	58.5	3,428	16	20
1968	3	—1	—.3	32	11	34.4	139	4	2
1969	11	23	2.1	327	178	54.4	2,342	20	12
1970	9	16	1.8	321	166	51.7	2,213	18	14
Totals	438	1,755	4.0	4,777	2,616	54.7	37,715	231	280

* Reprinted from THE BALTIMORE COLTS 1971 MEDIA GUIDE.